Mood Food

Caroline Shreeve is a doctor qualified in both conventional and alternative medicine. She is the author of several other books: *Divorce, Depression, The Premenstrual Syndrome* and *Cystitis* (published by Thorsons); *Overcoming the Menopause Naturally* and *The Alternative Dictionary of Symptoms and Cures* (published by Century). She lives in Wales.

CAROLINE SHREEVE

Mood Food

A Pan Original
Pan Books
London, Sydney and Auckland

First published 1988 by Pan Books Ltd,
Cavaye Place, London SW10 9PG
9 8 7 6 5 4 3 2 1
Copyright © Dr Caroline Shreeve
ISBN 0 330 30066 0

Printed in Great Britain by
Cox & Wyman Limited

This book is sold subject to the condition that it
shall not, by way of trade or otherwise, be lent, re-sold,
hired out, or otherwise circulated without the publisher's prior
consent in any form of binding or cover other than that in which
it is published and without a similar condition including this
condition being imposed on the subsequent purchaser

Contents

Introduction 1

Lighten Your Mood 27

Beat Your Stress 53

Increase Your Mind Power 83

Enjoy a Healthy and Active Old Age 111

Improve Your Physical Stamina and Pain Resistance 133

Boost Your Sexual Vigour 154

Put an End to Feminine Problems 174

Sources of Essential Nutrients 196

Recipe Index 201

For Jackie,
with love and thanks, for making me laugh so much.

Introduction

Throughout our lives, most of us come to associate certain types of food and drink with the way they make us feel. Sugary, starchy foods, for instance, are renowned for their buffering effects upon anxiety and misery. Comfort eaters, unlike the lovesick composer of the Song of Solomon who begged his listeners 'Comfort me with apples', almost invariably choose bars of chocolate, packets of biscuits, or toast and marmalade in times of need.

Likewise, most of us who have sat through a rich, heavy lunch on a working day will have experienced the intolerable drowsiness and poor concentration that such a meal can induce for several hours afterwards.

Numerous facts have come to light over the past decade about how certain nutrients, or a lack of them, affect our moods, emotions and intellectual performance, and there is now an increasing conviction among medical scientists that our moods can directly affect our physical health. The idea of holism lies at the foundation of the 'alternative' or complementary therapies, and modern orthodox medical thought is starting to pay serious attention to man as a 'whole' being, with interdependent physical, psychological and spiritual natures.

Emotional stress, tension and chronic anxiety, for instance, are now recognized as playing an important role in the generation of an increasingly wide range of diseases. Besides the familiar examples of strokes, heart attacks and high blood pressure, the list now includes peptic ulceration, the irritable bowel syndrome, diverticulitis, chronic digestive problems and migraine attacks. Certain types of cancer and autoimmune diseases such as rheumatoid arthritis, ulcerative colitis, and Crohn's disease are also thought to be stress-related, and researchers have now established that certain brain chemicals, produced when we are depressed or angry, increase our susceptibility to infectious illnesses.

Growing awareness among nutritional scientists of the complex interaction between mind and body has led them to explore the connections between diet and a wide range of human behaviour. A series of American studies has revealed that our choice both of diet and mealtimes, as well as our age and gender, influence our behaviour far more than was once believed.

How we sleep, whether we feel drowsy or alert, our response to stress, our experience of pain, whether we suffer from depressive illness, our work performance, our mood swings, and even our ability to stick to a slimming diet, can all be governed by what we eat and when we eat it.

The relationship between our diet and our moods and behaviour, is the fact that significant nutrient imbalance frequently produces emotional and behavioural symptoms before it produces gross physical symptoms and signs. There are many familiar examples; depression, mental stress, lowered physical stamina, irritability, childhood hyperactivity and impaired learning ability, and related conditions which have a direct bearing upon how we perform mentally and physically, and what type of mood we are in. These include senile confusion and intellectual impairment, pain perception, insomnia, a low libido (reduced interest in sex), and the emotional aspects of a number of women's complaints such as PMS, the menopause and painful periods.

The aim of this book is to show how choice of food can help to reverse unwanted conditions, relieve symptoms, and in some cases hopefully prevent them from developing.

Nutrition and Brain Power

The modern healthy diet should include complex carbohydrates with a high fibre content, and should aim to avoid a high total fat content, added sugar and salt. It also steers as clear as possible away from processed, refined foods, and obtains its protein content from vegetables, nuts, seeds and pulses, a little meat and fish, eggs and low fat dairy produce.

The basic principles of a truly healthy diet stem from a sound knowledge of the needs of all our bodily systems, since they are all interdependent and interfunctional. The healthy diet for each of us is that one best suited to our individual biochemical needs.

One day we may even arrive at a fully comprehensive holistic diet, which provides not only the nutrients our bodies require, but also foods that nourish us psychologically and spiritually as well. Soul nutrition recipes – incorporated into a total, holistic dietary framework – may well be with us before long!

The most complete eating pattern that can be achieved at present, though, is one that automatically takes care of the needs of your brain cells (and thereby your moods and behaviour), just as it caters for the special requirements of your kidneys, skin, lungs and reproductive organs. Once you supply your body with the nutrients it needs daily, in the balanced proportions it requires them, your brain will prove more than capable of extracting its fair share!

There is, however, a strong argument in favour of 'mood food'! Eating to adjust a tendency to depression, to overcome anxiety, or to treat period pains, menopausal symptoms or PMS in a natural, drug-free way, does not confine those who follow it to day after day of eating only those foods most suited to the needs of their brain cells, or of any other organ. Few people, anyway, would wax enthusiastic about eating, say, fish, yoghourt and broad beans, or yeast extract, bananas and brown rice for prolonged periods (which may well be the case if the requirements of only one bodily system were being considered).

The aim of 'mood food' advice and recipes is to allow anyone who chooses to stay, for example, alert, calm and able to cope, when faced with a tedious, after-lunch business meeting in a warm, stuffy office. Without knowing how moods and food interrelate, selecting the 'wrong' foods at lunchtime might well bring on irritability, sleepiness or depression. Knowing about mood and food can also be a social asset, whether you are giving a dinner party, or entertaining romantic notions for a dinner that is strictly 'à deux'! More information will be provided about dietary strategy in this and the following chapters.

The brain does, however, have certain unique nutritional needs which are worth knowing about. This makes it easier to understand some of the moods and emotional upsets that result when the brain's requirements are not being met. The brain also reacts by producing physical and emotional symptoms in response to conditions such as low blood sugar (hypoglycaemia), food allergy, a reduced level of the chemical serotonin in the brain (see Carbohydrate craving, page 6) and possibly poor utilization of vitamin A plus zinc deficiency (see Anorexia Nervosa, page 10). We will look at all these factors, before going on to consider healthy eating generally.

Glucose, Hypoglycaemia, Carbohydrate Craving, and Food Allergy

Although the activity of most bodily organs slows down during sleep, a constant source of energy has to be provided to enable them to remain 'on the go'. The brain, however, requires just as much fuel whether we are asleep, or pondering some deep mathematical problem at midday without the aid of a computer or pocket calculator.

Glucose

The most vital bodily fuel is glucose, which is derived from the sugars and starches in our diets, and is absorbed through the wall of the digestive tract, into the bloodstream. The circulating blood transports the glucose to every organ of the body but, whereas most organs are able to store a certain amount of glucose in their tissues in case supplies run short, the brain is unable to do so.

The cells of the brain are the first to suffer when the level of glucose in the blood falls below a certain level (about 80 milligrams of glucose per 100 millilitres of blood). Such a severe drop in blood glucose levels usually causes nausea, dizziness, and faintness. Levels below 25 mg/100 mls cause mental confusion and other neurological signs. Irreversible brain damage results if the levels drop below 10 mg/100 mls, and the comatose patient will die if he is not given an intravenous glucose infusion within a few seconds.

Because glucose is so vital to the brain, it has to be kept supplied with this nutrient at all costs. One of the reasons for its huge demand is the amount of energy the brain consumes in relation to its size. Although the adult brain weighs a mere 1,250–1,450 g, compared with a total body weight of between 60 and 70 kg, its activities account for twenty per cent of the body's total energy consumption. It needs 110 grams of glucose every twenty-four hours, and this amounts to some 450 calories. In order to 'burn' this fuel, it needs a constant supply of oxygen.

Hypoglycaemia

Hypoglycaemia is perhaps the best known condition that causes us to react emotionally to food. It is the low blood sugar many people have come to associate with the sudden onset of anxiety, panic attacks, weakness, irritability and sharp mood swings, as well as a long list of physical symptoms.

Hypoglycaemia can arise as a result of medical conditions such as diabetes, or insulinoma (a tumour of the pancreas or liver). The type of hypoglycaemia discussed here, however, is the 'reactive' type. Many articles have appeared about this in the popular press over the past three to four years, and as happens with many health scapegoats, it has been blamed for a vast variety of symptoms. Some writers on the subject are dismissive, saying that it is a rare condition. Others claim that it is far more common than most doctors realize, and that it is, therefore, frequently misdiagnosed and mistreated.

What is beyond dispute, is that the consumption of large quantities of refined carbohydrates can result in an upsurge of blood glucose levels, followed by the release of a hefty quantity of insulin into the blood by the pancreas. The theory put forward by those who support the 'reactive hypoglycaemia' theory, is that this insulin response is so strong that too much blood glucose is driven into the body cells, and the blood glucose drops severely.

People affected by hypoglycaemia find that their symptoms are alleviated by a sugary snack or sweet drink. The relief is short-lived, however, and the condition perpetuates itself since the fresh influx of sugar into the system creates part of a vicious circle.

What is not clear is the number of people this condition actually affects and why. Generally, vital biochemical parameters such as our body temperature, the acidity of our blood, the oxygen levels in our tissues and our blood glucose levels are kept in a state of almost perfect balance despite the challenges imposed by external environmental conditions, food intake etc. The probable truth is that some of us who are genetically more susceptible damage the delicate mechanism responsible for keeping our blood glucose levels within normal limits by abusing its ability to cope.

A major form of abuse is the habitual eating of large quantities of refined carbohydrate snacks, often from boredom, habit, misery or as a result of stress (see Carbohydrate craving, page 6). The risk of developing diabetes is believed to be increased by this eating pattern. Alcohol, too, can aggravate hypoglycaemia by inhibiting the activity of the hormone glucagon which regulates the amount of glucose in the blood.

The symptoms typically come on two to four hours after a high-sugar snack or meal. Many of the causes and their solutions you can handle yourself, but if simple dietary and lifestyle advice does not bring about a radical improvement, you should consult your doctor.

Start by altering your way of eating to a wholefood one with a high raw content. Give up junk food and sugary snacks, and take your carbohydrates in the form of the complex, unrefined variety with a high fibre content. Also avoid gaps of longer than two to three hours between meals or wholefood snacks. If your symptoms lessen and disappear, then you can gradually lengthen the time interval between eating to suit your needs.

You should also give up smoking and reduce your alcohol intake. Keep off the cigarettes for good. You can try gradually reintroducing small quantities of alcohol if you like. Monitor the effects, and get to know your own limits. It helps to drink on a full stomach, so have a wholefood snack before you drink. A glass of sparkling mineral water following every alcoholic drink you take, will also cut down the effect and make you less inclined to take too much alcohol. Anyway, reduce your alcohol intake to the safe limits of two 5 fl oz/150 ml glasses of wine daily, or their equivalent in beer, lager or spirits.

Try substituting the tea or coffee you drink with a herbal tea — there is sufficient variety of flavours available now to please most tastes. Learn to cope with stress by learning to relax. You can do this either by using a book or tape, or learning yoga or autogenics.

The vitamins that especially help to overcome hypoglycaemic symptoms include the B complex and C; and the most useful minerals are potassium, manganese, magnesium, chromium and zinc. Consult the table on page 196–200 to check on the best natural sources of these nutrients and try to include them daily in your wholefood diet.

Carbohydrate craving

Food cravings can mean that you have a food allergy (see page 7). Many non-allergic people hunger after carbohydrate foods, however, and eventually binge on them if they follow a diet that eliminates them altogether, or restricts them too severely.

Not all carbohydrate-cravers are obese. It depends upon their overall diet, the amount of exercise they take, and the rate at which they burn up food fuel (i.e. their metabolic rate). Many of them do suffer from mild to moderately severe depression, though, and this has been related to a lowered level of the neurotransmitter serotonin in the brain.

The amino acid tryptophan is necessary for the synthesis of serotonin. When carbohydrates are eaten, tryptophan is given preferential admission to the brain cells. It can then be converted into serotonin which reduces depression, and makes you feel relaxed and tranquil.

Women seen especially prone to carbohydrate craving, and as more women than men try to lose weight, the binge-diet-binge seesaw forms a serious obstacle for many of them. Stress increases the tendency to 'comfort eat', and PMS also produces carbohydrate cravings in the many women affected by it. The solution is to eat a balanced diet that incorporates sufficient carbohydrate to meet your personal needs.

Complex, unrefined carbohydrate snacks are useful as their high fibre content makes for a feeling of fullness and their sugar content is released slowly, avoiding an upsurge of blood glucose levels.

Food allergy

Food allergy is a true allergic reaction in which there is evidence of the production of antibodies in response to the suspected food or foods. This is the same type of allergic reaction as that which occurs in hay fever sufferers when they encounter pollen, and symptoms are triggered by the release of the chemical histamine from the affected tissues.

Food sensitivity is a state in which there is no evidence of an abnormal immunological response (no antibody production or histamine release), but in which a definite link is evident between food and symptoms.

The idea of certain foods and/or chemicals causing illness in particular people is becoming widely accepted. The orthodox medical profession first paid the concept proper attention after the work of American doctors Albert Rowe and Ted Randolph was made known in the 1920s and 1930s. They invented the elimination diet, which omits all foods of a certain kind from a patient's diet to discover whether the symptoms were relieved. They were able to tie up the disappearance of many chronic symptoms such as headaches, rheumatism, irritable bowel syndrome (spastic colon) and, in some cases, epilepsy and multiple sclerosis, with the elimination of one or several foods.

Since then, more and more people are coming to believe that unsuspected allergy may play a part in the generation of a growing number of diseases. The concept of cerebral allergy, however, which links an adverse reaction to certain foods and chemicals with mood, emotional disturbance and behavioural problems (as well as to headaches, and other neurological symptoms) is less widely accepted. It has nevertheless been established that some people do experience both physical and psychological reactions to foods to which they are allergic. An allergy to pork, for intance, gave one patient acute symptoms of food poisoning (severe stomach pains, neause, vomiting and diarrhoea), as well as panic attacks and feelings of acute anxiety and restlessness.

Where the symptoms are psychological and emotional only, the fact that food may be the underlying cause may never be suspected. A sensitivity to chocolate, for instance, has been linked with outbreaks of violently aggressive behaviour in susceptible people. Some experts now feel that food allergy or sensitivity may be responsible, not only for depression and rage in certain patients, but also for certain types of schizophrenia, hyperactivity, obsessive-compulsive behaviour, confusion and poor memory, inability to concentrate, anxiety and outbursts of violent behaviour.

Hyperactivity and bouts of aggressive behaviour in children have been linked with a sensitivity to wheat and milk, to certain food additives such as tartrazine, the synthetic yellow food colouring, and to the intake of refined sugar. Other pointers to a possible food allergy include food cravings and addiction – paradoxically to the very foods to which you are allergic – and hypoglycaemia.

The allergens (substances in food that trigger symptoms) differ widely from one individual to another. Egg yolk may cause confusion, poor memory and muscular weakness in one person, and intense irritability in another. Conversely, two people may experience the same symptoms in response to different dietary triggers. Susceptibility to the effects of one's personal food allergens is increased by the cumulative effect of all the toxic substances with which one is in contact, including atmospheric pollutants and other environmental toxins. Other factors include general state of health, the ability to cope with stress, the overall quality of the diet, alcohol consumption and cigarette smoking. Taking the contraceptive pill can increase one's tendency to food sensitivities, as can certain drugs, particularly tranquillizers and hypnotics (sleeping pills).

The simplest diagnostic test is to exclude all the foods to which you think you may possibly be allergic. You avoid the suspect foods altogether for four days, then reintroduce them *one at a time* every four days, stopping one before starting the next and thereby never eating the suspected substances in combination. Frequent offenders include milk and milk products, beef, pork and chicken, hen's eggs, sugar, coffee and tea, chocolate, oranges, synthetic food additives and yeast-containing foods. Recurrence of symptoms can often be linked with a particular food or foods by this method.

The adverse effects of monosodium glutamate (MSG) should also be remembered. This is a food additive much used in Chinese cooking for its properties as a flavour enhancer. Allergic responses have been well documented, and the illness it causes is known as the 'Chinese restaurant syndrome'. This is characterized by severe headaches, and a generalized feeling of being very unwell.

The best treatment of food allergy is avoidance of the culprit foods. Sometimes they can be reintroduced in small quantities without adverse reactions, after they have been avoided entirely for two to three months. Avoid going overboard about them, though, and continue to take them only occasionally and in small quantities.

Basic common-sense health measures – well worth following for their own sake – are known to decrease your susceptibility to food allergies. They include taking regular exercise, as often as possible in fresh, country air; learning to relax and cope with stress; ceasing to smoke and to take alcohol in large quantities; avoiding all forms of medication that are not absolutely necessary (ask your doctor first about prescribed medicines); and eating a strictly whole food diet that eliminates all forms of junk food and additives.

By eating as much raw food as possible, you will be helping yourself to the vitamins and minerals you need in their natural forms. Raw foods also offer some protection against the damaging effects of environmental toxins. Pay special attention to the B complex vitamins, A, and C, and make sure by checking with the Table on page 196–200 that you include adequate supplies of foods containing manganese (essential for carbohydrate metabolism) and zinc.

You should consult a nutritional specialist about severe or prolonged food allergy symptoms. He or she may suggest a natural vitamin, mineral or amino acid supplement to your health diet.

Vitamins, Minerals and Other Nutrients

The brain's need of oxygen is just as great as its need for glucose. Deprivation of oxygen for even a few minutes causes brain damage and death. The blood supply to the brain has a unique feature with a direct bearing upon the supply of nutrients reaching it. This is known as the blood-brain barrier, and refers to the filtering property of the brain's blood vessels, which permit certain nutrients in the bloodstream to reach the brain cells, yet excludes others. The effects of the blood-brain barrier on brain nutrition will be discussed further in connection with amino acid brain nutrients.

In common with every other organ, the brain needs proteins, carbohydrates, fats and other major dietary items. In particular it needs certain vitamins and minerals which act as 'helpers' for the work it does, receiving, interpreting and transmitting electrical nerve impulses both from one area of itself to another, and to and from the rest of the body. In addition, the cells of the brain are constantly engaged in the process of internal maintenance. Worn out dendrites and neuronal sheaths require repair, and hormones and neurotransmitters need to be manufactured to keep up their supply.

Essential vitamins include the B complex, C, choline, inositol, biotin (vitamin H), and vitamin M (folic acid), and there are probably others. Vital minerals include sodium, potassium, iron, magnesium, zinc, sulphur, iodine (indirectly), and copper.

Anorexia nervosa

Anorexia nervosa is slimming taken to such extreme limits that a profoundly serious weight loss is experienced. Most of the body's accessible stored fat is used up by the body's need for glucose and calories, and the muscle protein is metabolized to provide energy, causing the loss of lean muscle mass. A sense of distorted perception often occurs, so that the patient perceives herself to be grotesquely fat and overweight however much the scales prove the contrary.

Psychological problems have always been believed to lie at the centre of anorexia nervosa and its 'twin' complaint, bulimia nervosa, in which the sufferer frequently binges on vast quantities of food but vomits in private in order to avoid putting on weight. However, it is now thought that malfunction of the pituitary gland, may be a contributory factor and it has also been suggested that an inability to utilize vitamin A and a deficiency of zinc may be important aspects of the cause of anorexia nervosa. Both complaints are commoner in teenagers than adults. Girls and women are much more likely to be affected than men.

The All Purpose Healthy Diet

Given the basic principles of healthy eating mentioned earlier, opinion still differs radically among nutritionally conscious people regarding the 'best' diet to follow. The three most important diets that should be mentioned here, are wholefood, vegetarian and vegan. Followers of each of these ways of eating, and 'average omnivores' (people who eat anything they enjoy), were compared in a 1985 nutritional study in the UK to discover which came closest to the 'ideal' diet.

A detailed report of the findings appeared in the July 1985 issue of the *Journal of Alternative Medicine*. Many people were interested to note that the vegan group – who consume no animal products of any kind, and who are most often criticized for eating in an unbalanced way – came closest to achieving optimum nutrition.

Although this book does not specify either a vegan or a vegetarian approach to eating, it does support the steadily growing belief among many nutritional experts that most people eat far more protein than they need.

The diet suggested in this book is a wholefood one, with an emphasis on obtaining protein from vegetable sources, rather than from meat or fish, although both are included. This approach allows far more latitude of choice in planning menus, shopping, cooking and entertaining – as well as eating out. Few people who enjoy meat are prepared to give it up altogether, and with a little judicious juggling it is quite possible to eat – not only your cake – but also the occasional small fillet steak (grilled with a fine film of cold-pressed vegetable oil, naturally, rather than fried in butter!)

The basis of the wholefood diet is that it consists of food that is as close to its 'whole' state as possible, with nothing taken away from it, and nothing added. While this immediately outlaws the hundreds of everyday processed convenience foods that are so easy to thaw, de-can, rehydrate, reconstitute, or 'grill or boil from frozen in a plastic bag', it does not necessarily involve you in spending longer in the kitchen than you do already.

Wholefood recipes have travelled light years from their earlier forbidding image of grey, lustreless heaps of powdery wholewheat pasta or boiled lentils, accompanied by unidentifiable sauces. Wholefood and vegetarian cookery writers such as Janette Marshall, Sarah Brown, Rose Elliot, Miriam Polunin, and Leslie and Susannah Kenton have shown how attractive and economical a healthy diet can be. Thousands of people use their recipes, not simply because the ingredients and cookery methods are superior nutritionally, but because eating whole foods reawakens the taste-buds to how food can and should taste.

Research carried out over the past decade has also indicated the advantages of a diet containing a high proportion of raw food.

The Kentons, in their best selling book *Raw Energy* (Century Publishing Company, 1985), presented much evidence for the beneficial effects of 'high raw' eating, not only upon general health but also upon mood, stress responses, anxiety levels, mental alacrity, behaviour and emotions. The Kentons include high proportions of fresh fruit, vegetables, nuts, seeds and sprouts in their dietary approach. They point out the advantages it offers to sportsmen, athletes and anyone whose lifestyle requires huge physical stamina. Doctor Barbara Moore is a familiar name to many, as a lady who walked marathon distances on the energy she obtained from carrot juice. Leslie and Susannah also mention George Allen, holder of the record for walking from John O'Groats to Land's End, who kept going day and night during his walk, and lived on raw vegetables. They also mention how Maurice Mességué, the well-known herbalist, 'trained the racing cyclists Fausto Coppi and Luis

Ocana to victory on a strict routine of raw fruits and vegetables, whole grains and honey'.

Carbohydrates

Carbohydrates evoke a fair amount of controversy. Since this food class includes starch and sugar, and since carbohydrates play a significant part in wholefood eating, many would-be slimmers shy away from this approach on the grounds that they could never lose weight. However, this is not a valid criticism, as Audrey Eyton's best-selling *F Plan Diet* (Penguin, 1982) conclusively proved. The type of carbohydrates wholefood eating includes are the complex, unrefined variety with a high, natural fibre content, that make you feel full and satisfied without involving a high calorie count. Most nutritional experts agree that about 60–70 per cent of a healthy adult's diet should consist of unrefined, 'whole' carbohydrates.

In place of denatured white flour, wholefooders use wholemeal flour. This is produced by milling the whole wheat grain including the fibrous bran, and the wheatgerm which provides essential fatty acids and vitamins B and E, calcium and iron. Bread, pasta, cakes, biscuits, roux and sauces can all be made successfully from wholemeal flour. 'Eighty-one per cent' wholemeal flour is available for recipes requiring an especially delicate touch, such as sponges and choux pastry. This is simply wholemeal flour from which some of the bran has been removed.

Other unrefined carbohydrates favoured by wholefood eaters include root vegetables; grains such as rice (the brown variety), barley, maize or corn, oats, rye, wheat, millet, and buckwheat (strictly speaking, a seed); and pulses (dried beans, peas and lentils). These foods are also rich in protein, and many are valuable sources of vitamins, minerals and unsaturated vegetable oil.

Regarding the vexed question of sugar, it is true that the wholefood diet adds very little extra sweetness to dishes. Nevertheless, many sceptics of this way of eating are pleasantly surprised at how sweet many 'whole' cakes, pies, biscuits, tarts and desserts turn out to be. Wholefood recipes favour the inclusion of sliced or grated raw fruit, chopped dried fruit, fruit concentrates, or grated, naturally sweet vegetables such as parsnips and carrots, to sweeten dishes.

There is nothing new about this approach. Vegetables with a high content of natural sugar have been used for centuries to add sweetness to puddings and cakes. Early recipes for steamed puddings, in particular Christmas pudding, frequently included grated carrot for the natural sweetness and moisture it provided.

Where a higher sugar content is needed, wholefood recipes make use of unrefined sugar such as demerara or Barbados, or perhaps honey, maple syrup or molasses. Meringues work well if you substitute fine, soft brown sugar (or closely ground demerara), for the usual white caster variety, especially if you reduce the moisture content of the sugar by placing it in a thin layer on a baking tray, and leaving it in a warm, switched off oven for half an hour with the door ajar. It should be cooled to room temperature before it is used.

Fibre

Dietary fibre is derived from the cell walls of plants. Wholemeal flour and foods made from it, whole grains, pulses, vegetables and fruits, seeds and nuts provide it in plenty, and a simple way of ensuring that you get sufficient is to include as much raw fruit and vegetables in your diet as possible.

There are several different types of fibre, all with slightly different effects upon the body. The main varieties are cellulose (present in the husks of cereal crops), lignin (found in mature root vegetables such as parsnips and carrots, and the outer leaves of cabbages and cauliflowers), pectin (found in most fruit), and gums.

Cellulose fibre or bran (e.g. from wheat, oats) is especially helpful in ending constipation. Food and its ultimate waste products pass through the bowel more rapidly, because the fibre absorbs water and forms a soft bulky mass. The presence of this inside the bowel stimulates its muscles to squeeze its contents along more rapidly and effectively. This helps useful bowel bacteria to flourish at the expense of harmful varieties and reduces the risk of toxic food breakdown products damaging the intestinal lining.

Oat bran is especially helpful, since, unlike wheat bran, it contains no phytic acid. This substance tends to bind with minerals, particularly calcium ions, thereby affecting their absorption by the body.

Pectin is water soluble, but it is not digested and it softens stools by increasing their water content. Lignin binds with bile salts and offers some protection against gall stone formation. It also lowers the blood level of the kinds of lipids (fats) that play a part in the 'furring up' effect seen in ageing arteries.

The recommended daily intake for fibre in the UK is between 25 and 30 grams. This is believed to help guard against a number of disorders such as diverticulitis, cancer of the large bowel, certain hernias, piles (haemorrhoids), gallstones, obesity (you are more satisfied with less food because of its greater bulk, and having to chew it more thoroughly helps satiate hunger pangs), peptic ulceration, high blood pressure, varicose veins and certain forms of cardiovascular disorders.

Diabetics benefit from a high-fibre diet for reasons which are relevant to brain cells in general. Food with a high fibre content is digested more slowly than refined carbohydrates (such as a Mars bar) and glucose is released at a slow and steady rate, preventing the sudden surges and drops in blood glucose levels associated with diabetes and hypoglycaemia (page 5).

Protein

For many people, the word protein conjures up an image of a massive side of roast beef, underdone to a turn, with an attractive brown outer covering of skin, a thin layer of fat, and an interior that becomes steadily pinker as the centre is approached. While this and other red meats are an excellent source of first class protein, however, nutritional experts warn us against the inclusion of too much red meat in our diets.

The disadvantages of meat – especially red meat – are its high saturated fat content, believed to contribute to the development of cardiovascular disease; the presence of drug residues and growth-inducing hormones, and the possible link between beef meat and fat, and certain types of intestinal cancer. In addition, meat products such as sausages, mince, meat pies and beefburgers generally contain colouring, preservatives, artificial flavourings and other synthetic additives. Meat and meat products also lack beneficial fibre.

Wholefood advocates generally turn for their protein supplies to white fish (which contains unsaturated fat and helps to protect against heart and arterial disease), free-range poultry, low-fat cheese, up to three free-range eggs per week, yeast extract, and pulses, seeds and grains. Chick peas (a type of pulse) are rich in protein. Nuts (especially peanuts) and seeds are high in proteins and fats, and supply a good range of vitamins and minerals. The grains have already been discussed as excellent sources of complex carbohydrates, fibre and protein. Vegetable proteins also provide fewer calories than animal proteins.

All tissues of the body require protein. Besides energy, which protein provides at the same rate as sugar or starch, i.e. just over four calories per gram, protein foods supply the basic building blocks from which bodily tissues build and repair their structures and compounds. These processes continue throughout life, as old cells die and are replaced with new. For this, amino acids (the structural units of which all protein is composed) are required.

Protein taken into the body is digested in the stomach and small bowel. It is broken down into simpler compounds known as peptides, and these in turn are further broken down into the basic amino acid units. In this form, they pass to the bloodstream and travel to the liver. Here they are resynthesized into the proteins the body requires.

There are about twenty amino acids, and twelve of these are 'non-essential' (i.e. the body manufactures them itself), in contrast to the remaining eight essential ones which must be provided by our diet. Both groups are needed, and all the EAAs have to be present in the digestive tract at any one time for protein synthesis to occur. Protein foods such as red meat are termed 'first class' proteins because they contain all the EAAs; vegetable proteins are known as 'second class' proteins because they do not.

However, vegetable protein sources can be combined in the diet in such a way that the full complement of EAAs is obtained. Non-animal proteins fall into three groups according to the amino acids they contain – cereals, pulses and nuts. By combining any two groups at one meal, all the amino acids can be obtained. This is just as satisfactory as eating a first-class protein meal.

The recommended daily intake for protein in the UK is 65 to 90 grams for men, and 55 to 63 for women. Certain factors increase our need for protein, among them excessive heat, infection and stress. Further variables include age (growing children need more protein per unit body weight than adults), occupation (heavy manual jobs create a greater need than sedentary ones), and biological individuality.

If our total intake of calories is too low to meet our needs over a prolonged period, our need for protein will also increase. This is because the body will convert protein, derived either from the diet or from its own tissues, into glucose, rather than allow the blood glucose level to fall dangerously low. Wastage of lean body tissues is one of the serious dangers of trying to lose weight on a very low calorie diet.

Paradoxically, eating too much protein can result in a deficiency of amino acids which can have an extremely serious effect upon brain function, emotions, behaviour and mood, and which works in the following way. Large quantities of dietary protein can overtax the pancreas. Other factors such as excessive amounts of dietary fat, sugar, alcohol and coffee, cigarette smoking and the use of a wide range of drugs also affect the pancreas. It becomes less efficient at producing the hormone insulin and the digestive enzymes, so the proteins fail to be broken down into amino acids as they should. An amino acid deficiency therefore results.

The brain depends upon amino acids, not only for repair operations, but also for manufacturing hormones, enzymes and – most importantly in the context of mood and emotions – neurotransmitters (the chemical messengers in the brain). When the amino acids reach the blood-brain barrier, they are sorted into their three basic types, acidic, alkaline ('basic') and neutral. A separate means of entry exists for each of these, but only a certain number of any one type are admitted at any particular time.

For this reason, they vie with one another to gain entry, acidic types competing with other acidic types, neutral amino acids with other neutral amino acids and so on. In certain cases, it is possible to give a particular amino acid an advantage over others in its group, by increasing the level of it in the blood.

The neutral amino acid tryptophan is important here. Low blood levels of tryptophan are associated with depression, and this has been related to a correspondingly low level in the brain of the neurotransmitter serotonin, into which tryptophan is changed by the brain cells. In many cases, depression has been successfully treated by increasing the amount of tryptophan taken in the diet. Lack of tryptophan also leads to a craving for carbohydrate foods, and supplements have been used as an aid both to weight loss and also to obtaining better quality sleep.

Fat

A wholefood diet favours the use of polyunsaturated fats and oils of vegetable origin, in preference to the use of saturated animal fat. It also aims at keeping the total quantity of fat consumed low. There is no actual recommended daily intake of fats in the UK in terms of weight. However, nutritional expert Professor Roy Walford suggests that an ideal dietary regimen for a healthy adult between the ages of twenty and fifty should include less than 10 to 15 per cent fat. He feels that it could be whittled down even further, to the region of 2 to 5 per cent without causing a fatty acid deficiency. People over the age of fifty years, the Professor feels, are most likely to benefit from a fat intake of around 10 to 15 per cent.

The best sources of polyunsaturated fats (PUFAs) are safflower oil and soya bean oil for cooking and cold sauces; corn oil, sunflower seed oil and olive oil, and certain nut oils are also good. Foods supplying useful amounts of PUFAs include soya flour, nuts and seeds (e.g. sunflower seeds, pumpkin seeds). All fats provide just over nine calories of energy per gram. With refined carbohydrates, fats are really the dieter's worst enemy, and this applies as much to margarine as to butter, as their energy value is identical.

Saturated fats and cholesterol were first considered to be partly responsible for cardiovascular disease in the early 1950s. The human body makes its own cholesterol (a type of body lipid or fat) and, since this substance is found in the fatty (atheromatous) plaques on the walls of diseased arteries, it was felt that people should be advised to reduce their intake of both cholesterol and saturated (animal) fat. Very many experts still believe this view to be correct, but others feel that there is insufficient supporting evidence.

Professor Walford falls into the latter group. He points out that since this nutritional policy was put into practice, heart disease has remained the number one killer. Other figures support the opposite view, of course, and while controversy rages, it is still safer to substitute fats derived from animals with plant and vegetable oil. All the same, it is only fair to mention that an increase in cases of cancer has been noted in connection with dietary regimens that substitute vegetable oil for butter, and that there seems to be a decreased number of cardiovascular deaths among people whose blood cholesterol levels have been lowered by a diet high in PUFAs.

One cannot deduce from this either that saturated animal fats are safe, or that PUFAs give you cancer. The message really is that neither one nor the other should be taken in excess, and that cutting down your total intake of fats and oils from all sources is a very wise dietary move.

A point in favour of the PUFAs is their content of vitamin E and essential fatty acids (EFAs). However, always choose 'cold pressed' vegetable oils, and margarine made from these. They are harder to find and usually more expensive, but the cold pressing process leaves the resultant oil chemically uncontaminated with the greater part of its useful nutrients intact. Manufacturing processes that do not use cold pressing generally involve the use of high temperatures that chemically affect the oil, destroying much of its vitamins and altering its EFA, cis-linoleic acid, into an 'anti-vitamin' known as trans-linoleic acid. Margarine made from heat-treated oils also contains synthetic colouring matter, preservatives, emulsifiers and flavourings.

The body uses – and stores – fats as a source of energy, and as a means of repairing damaged cell membranes. It also needs them to manufacture a wide range of hormones and vital chemicals, including a group known as the prostaglandins, hormone-like substances responsible for controlling the minute-by-minute metabolic activities of the cells throughout the body, including those of the brain.

The brain uses fat and cholesterol for repair and maintenance; it does not seem to make use of them as a source of energy. The EFA, cis-linoleic acid, is vital for repair to brain cells, and a gross deficiency of it is associated with poor coordination, confusion, hallucinations and loss of memory.

In addition, the EFA into which cis-linoleic acid is converted in the body – GLA, or gammalinolenic acid – has been used successfully in the treatment of many disorders. It affords protection against the damaging effects of excessive amounts of alcohol on the liver. GLA (present in evening primrose oil, Efamol) has also been used to treat schizophrenia and PMS. Many women have found that Efamol relieves the tension, irritability and depression that are common features of this condition.

Vitamins, Minerals and Trace Elements

We have been made far more aware over the past two decades of the vital roles that vitamins and many minerals play in human biochemistry. Many of us turn to B vitamins to protect us from the effects of stress, and to vitamin C in the hope that it will increase our resistance to infectious illnesses. But for these measures to be effective we need to understand the interdependence of dietary vitamins and minerals. All of them need to be included in our diets in the 'correct' proportions, not only to our individual requirements but also to one another.

Vitamin C affords a good example of this. Many people take a gram a day when winter approaches or when they feel that they are developing a cold. Not everyone knows, however, that because this water soluble vitamin is excreted in two to three hours (depending upon the quality and quantity of food in the stomach), supplements should be taken in a time-release form. This helps to ensure that a constant high level of vitamin C is maintained in the bloodstream all the time the supplement is being taken.

In addition, if you take more than 750 mg of vitamin C daily you should also supplement your magnesium intake, as this helps to reduce the risk of developing kidney stones.

It is also a fact that natural vitamins are more beneficial than their synthetic counterparts. Chemical analysis of both might suggest that the naturally derived and laboratory produced forms of any vitamin are exactly similar to one another. However, the natural variety is much less likely to cause toxic side effects, and generally contains other nutrients important to their desired effect in the body. Synthetic vitamin C, for example, is simply ascorbic acid. Natural vitamin C, by contrast, is derived from rosehips and contains the entire vitamin C complex and bioflavonoids as well.

It follows from this that obtaining a large part of our vitamins and minerals from natural dietary sources rather than from tablets in a bottle, is the best possible way of giving our bodies the nutrients they require. Extra supplements can be added to 'top up' our total daily intake, but these should always be in naturally occurring forms.

Apart from the clearly toxic substances, such as lead and aluminium, it is a general rule that either an excess or a deficiency of any dietary nutrient is harmful, and that it is the quantities of them in the body in relation to one another and to the individual's needs, that give them their useful or noxious qualities.

Table salt, for instance, shunned by the health conscious today as contributive to raised blood pressure and heart disease contains the vital cation sodium. If this was completely absent from the diet, metabolic disaster and death would occur. There is nothing intrinsically harmful about either the sodium or the chloride components of this common substance. What is injurious about it is the excessive quantities we eat, over and above our metabolic requirements.

Drugs

Tea and coffee

Both contain the drug caffeine, as also do Pepsi and Coca Cola, chocolate and cocoa, and a number of pain killers. A twelve-ounce can of Coca Cola contains 64.7 mg caffeine, Pepsi just over two thirds of this amount. Instant coffee provides around 66.0 mg per serving, and percolated coffee, 110.0 mg. Tea bags that require five minutes to brew give you 46.0 mg caffeine per cup, and one-minute tea bags give you 28.0. Cocoa provides less per serving, at 13.0 mg per cup.

Caffeine helps other analgesic drugs to relieve pain, and lessens fatigue. It clears the head, and increases alertness. This effect is partly due to the fact that it releases glucose stored in the liver, thereby elevating the blood glucose level and feeding the brain with an extra source of energy.

However, it causes nerviness and anxiety, irritability, poor sleep, and depression, and suppresses the appetite. It also depresses the absorption of zinc, and can induce a deficiency of this mineral.

Alcohol

This is the most widely used drug in Western society. It appears to give you a lift because it damps down anxiety and combats tension and worries. What it is actually doing is to depress the brain's 'higher centres' of control in the cerebral cortex, thereby removing inhibitions and an awareness of social restrictions (when taken in sufficiently large amounts, that is). It also helps to destroy the brain's neurones by removing water from them, and can cause hypoglycaemia (see page 5). In addition, alcohol depletes the body of vitamins B1, 2, 6 and 12, folic acid, vitamin C and vitamin K, and of magnesium, calcium, zinc and potassium.

How we react to alcohol, long-term, depends upon such factors as our daily diet, whether we smoke, how we cope with stress (as well as how much stress we encounter), and our overall nutritional status. When you drink is as important as what you drink. Alcohol consumed between 2 a.m. and noon, stays in the blood far longer than the same quantity drunk during the late afternoon or early evening. The longer alcohol remains in the bloodstream, the greater its opportunity to affect the brain cells, as well as those of many other organs. You may have noticed how a pre-dinner drink or several glasses of wine taken with your evening meal, merely make you pleasantly relaxed, whereas alcohol taken at lunch time, even when accompanied by food, makes you drowsy for several hours afterwards.

Cigarette smoking

In addition to the well-known association between smoking and cancer and cardiovascular disease, smoking also depletes the body of vitamin C, at the rate of about 25 mg of the vitamin per cigarette. It may also have an adverse effect upon the B complex vitamins. It certainly impairs the function of the pancreas, and this may indirectly affect mood and behaviour.

The Diet in Practice

It is one thing to accept that a particular way of eating has distinct advantages over one's present choice of diet. It is another thing entirely to change one's eating habits accordingly, equipped, as most of us are, with a built-in mental blueprint of the week's needs, starting off with, say, 'a jar of X brand coffee, one pack of eighty tea-bags, and three loaves of bread', and ending somewhere in the region of 'ten tins of cat food, six loo rolls and half a pint of double cream'.

We create blueprints because they serve a need, and however well we may be motivated towards changing our lives, and improving our physical and emotional health, it is somehow always the built-in plan of 'what has worked in the past' — even if inefficiently — that continues to reign.

Here, then, is some practical advice about how to eat real wholefood sensibly, economically, and above all enjoyably.

Breakfast

Many of us already eat starchy food for breakfast. It is quick and easy to prepare, and although it may well not be the best choice for some (as we will see later on), quickly prepared, healthy breakfasts are for many people a great improvement on the 'cup of black coffee and a bar of chocolate on the train' syndrome, or the 'I never need anything until lunchtime' state of mind.

You are either a muesli fan already or you are not. One firm marketing a popular brand, voiced the opinion of many sceptical members of their target market by quoting an assessment of another (longer established) brand of muesli — 'a plateful of cold porridge'. If this verdict reflects *your* experience of muesli so far, take heart. The popular brands tend to be over-crisped and over-sweetened, and to promise far more deliciousness in the illustration on the packet than they can support in the experience of their contents. 'Real' muesli can be made easily and cheaply at home, or bought at a reasonable price in health food shops that frequently make up their own versions.

Add natural yoghourt or fruit juice to the muesli, or a little skimmed milk. If you have a very sweet tooth, it may seem in urgent need of a tablespoonful or three of honey or brown sugar — but be patient! It takes time (surprisingly little) to lose the need for very sweet foods, and once you have lost it, highly sweetened products seem nauseatingly over-sugared. This change in your taste buds is a great health asset.

Fresh fruit, fruit purée or a fruit compôte are also good ideas — with or without muesli, depending on time and appetite. If you must have animal protein for breakfast; change your present predilection for green back rashers, mushrooms and fried bread for a free-range boiled or poached egg, with a slice of whole grain bread, lightly toasted. Add a mere scraping of PUFA-margarine if you really must.

Lunch (or Evening Meal)

A large salad daily is a very good idea indeed. Include as many root and leaf vegetables are you can lay your hands on! – and add sprouted seeds and grains, fruit, and nuts or pulses. With the exception of raw potato, which really doesn't have much appeal, try grating turnips, swede or parsnip, carrots and raw beetroot. Chopped radishes and salsify are also delicious. Grate rather than chop a section of a large onion for extra juiciness, and use the leaves of cauliflower, winter and spring cabbage, Chinese lettuce and summer lettuce when they are worth buying and have some flavour. Cos lettuce, especially the heart, chopped and mixed with celery heart and grated fennel, makes a very pleasant mixture.

The fruit content can be practically anything you have to hand. A few segments of ripe orange, thinly sliced apple (with its skin), a few seeded grapes or half a sliced, juicy pear add interesting flavours. Mix in some sprouted mung beans (bean shoots), alfalfa shoots or mustard and cress which you can grow for a few pence on your window sill. Add a sprinkling of chopped walnuts, Brazil nuts or unsalted peanuts. If you can find them (and afford them), macadamia nuts are delicious and filling.

Evening Meal – or Main Midday Meal

Make sure you include your protein in this meal, whether you choose to combine nuts, grains or pulses as its source, or eggs, a little lean meat, fish or poultry. You will find plenty of ideas for main meal dishes, as well as for salads, among the recipes in this book.

You can make sure of eating a reasonably high-raw diet by including a salad with your main meal as a side dish. Finish the meal with some fresh fruit, yoghourt, or a dessert made with wholefood ingredients.

Snacks and Drinks

Widen the scope of your usual drinks by trying out freshly squeezed vegetable and fruit juices, recipes for which you will find later in the book. An electric centrifuge juicer is a very great asset here, as you can then use any vegetable or fruit you choose. There are many different mineral waters in the shops now, and the naturally effervescent ones, served with ice and a twist of lemon or lime peel, are a healthy and refreshing alternative to wine, beer, spirits and hot beverages.

If you must have tea and coffee, try China tea served without sugar or milk, or a herbal tea, and select a decaffeinated instant or percolated coffee. Dandelion coffee has an interesting flavour. Low-salt yeast extract drinks and natural vegetable stock cubes make a warming and satisfying mid-morning drink.

A variety of snack suggestions appear in the recipe section. Fresh fruit, a little dried fruit, unsalted nuts or seeds, and wholefood snacks made from grains and dried fruit are all healthy alternatives to bars of chocolate, biscuits made from refined ingredients, crisps and doughnuts.

Recipes and Meal Suggestions

The recipes and meal suggestions in *Mood Food* are intended to highlight particular ways of eating which, if incorporated into a long-term choice of diet, should help you to deal effectively with various nutrient-related conditions. All of them should be viewed against their essential background of a healthy and balanced wholefood diet. None of them purports to be either a 'wonder cure' for a particular condition, or an alternative to medical treatment whenever this may be required.

I must also point out that few of them are likely to show any effect if you only use them on the odd occasion. Altering your present way of eating to the type of meals indicated in the various sections, though, may prove very beneficial over a period of even a few weeks. The range of different foods appropriate to any particular problem allows for a far wider selection of meals and snacks than I have space to indicate here. Turn to the 'Which Foods?' part of each chapter to check the ingredients that supply what you need for a particular effect, and make your own choices.

I should also point out the inevitable overlap that exists between the nutrients designed to combat the various mood and emotional problems. Most nutrients have numerous and complex functions in the body and brain, and for this reason crop up time and again in the lists of nutrients required for various purposes.

You will also find that most of the recipes contain ingredients that are not specifically related to the mood or emotional problem in question. This is inevitable, considering the nature of the reactions we are dealing with. All the foods included qualify as 'whole' and healthy, and the salt, for those who prefer to include it, is the low sodium type. Whenever you are able, try to choose meat, vegetables, poultry and other produce that have been organically reared, and free-range eggs.

The breakfasts I suggest are aimed at speed of preparation (as well as taste!), and I have included protein meals among them, while steering clear of the traditional English fried version of this meal. I have made lunch a light meal, and the evening meal a more substantial one as this seems to suit most people. However, they are interchangeable to suit your own needs.

I have also thought of most midday meals as rather hurried affairs snatched while 'on the job', i.e. packed lunches taken to work, or quick meals to prepare while busy at home. For this reason, they consist in the main of soups, salads, sandwiches and finger snacks. I also suggest what to choose if you eat out in a pub or canteen in the middle of the day.

In dealing with the cooked evening meal, I give recipes in each section for one vegetarian dish, one based on fish, one based on meat, and one slightly more elaborate one for entertaining. I am assuming that most people eat puddings and desserts occasionally, although few find the time to make them every day. For this reason, I suggest light, easily prepared desserts for rounding off weekday meals, based on fresh fruit, fruit tinned in juice, yoghourt and milk. Recipes for more substantial desserts can be found in the dinner party menus.

All the recipes are for one, unless indicated otherwise.

Lighten Your Mood

Depression is a common condition in Western countries. According to a study by the National Institute of Mental Health in America, up to fifteen per cent of all adults may suffer depressive symptoms of varying degrees of severity in any given year.

Everyone succumbs to feeling 'blue' occasionally, but depressive illness is more than this. It is characterized by feelings of worthlessness, despair and often great anxiety, and makes life extremely difficult to cope with. It becomes very difficult to concentrate, and many sufferers complain of the difficulty of going on from day to day with job, domestic duties and family life, while unable to feel that there is any point in attempting to make efforts of any kind.

There are two main varieties of neurotic depression, that is depression in which a sense of reality, however painful, is retained. (I am not dealing in this book with psychotic depression nor any other type of psychotic illness, in which the patient experiences delusional states, illusions and hallucinations.) They are reactive (arising in the main from external factors), and endogenous (arising from within). Precipitating factors include poor health and diet, stress, and traumatic 'life events' — in themselves serious stress factors. Disorders of neurotransmission within the brain, affecting the neurotransmitters serotonin and noradrenaline known to be associated with mood and emotions, also play a major role in many cases of depressive illness. A further biochemical defect that may play a part in neurotic depression is inefficiency of the sodium pumps in the body's cell membranes. This results in an increase in cellular sodium levels significantly beyond the normal level.

The onset of endogenous depression cannot usually be traced back to a particular event. It seems to arise for no apparent reason, and this 'causelessness' to the mind of the person suffering from it is yet another form of torment. Many moderately to severely depressed people consult their GPs or alternative therapists stating that they feel that they are going mad. In fact this is not the case, but it is easy to understand why the belief arises. 'How can I possibly feel *this* purposeless, desperate, and despairing', some depressed people ask, 'when my life on the outside at least, is fine, and the envy of my friends?'

Sufferers from the reactive form of the illness, however, can frequently trace their illness back to a particular event in their lives. This may be bereavement, the termination of a love affair, a miscarriage or abortion, divorce, redundancy, sudden serious financial loss or a combination of several such emotional body blows. Instead of recovering, though, as non-depressed people eventually do, given the time to mourn and/or to reorganize their lives, someone suffering from reactive depression continues to suffer mentally. Life experience becomes one long sense of bereavement, and they become convinced that they will never feel any different.

Both forms of neurotic depression can entail physical as well as emotional symptoms. Speech and movement are often noticeably slower, and sleep disturbances are common. People suffering from the reactive variety, generally experience considerable difficulty in getting to sleep at night. Once asleep, though, they usually sleep until the alarm wakes them. Endogenously depressed people often get to sleep without a problem, only to be inflicted with 'early morning waking'. This can interrupt sleep a couple of hours before dawn, a very irritating experience when the oblivion of sleep is sometimes the only respite the person has from mental suffering. It can, on the other hand, waken the depressed person only an hour or two after he or she has dozed off. This can mean three or four hours of restless tossing and turning, and is an understandably common cause for requests for sleeping tablets.

In addition to the inevitable fatigue such sleep disturbances cause, depression frequently affects the appetite, and causes digestive upsets and constipation. It makes the reactions sluggish so that it seems to take twice as long as normal to perform simple tasks, especially those that require thought, and it is often associated with reduced sexual desire and impaired performance, menstrual irregularities and headaches.

Which Foods?

The amino acid **tryptophan** is the starter substance from which the brain neurotransmitter serotonin is made. As we saw on page 7, brain levels of serotonin are often low in sufferers from depression, so foods which supply tryptophan are likely to help lighten mood. Its free entry into the brain is ensured by carbohydrate-rich foods.

Five of the foods richest in tryptophan are lamb, liver, roast beef, pumpkin seeds and trout. Chicken breast, cod, shrimps, roasted peanuts and sesame seeds provide a good supply, and others worth remembering for their tryptophan content are soya flour, cottage cheese, brazil nuts, skimmed milk and soya beans.

A good plan is to eat a protein meal with as high a tryptophan content as you can, followed a couple of hours later by a carbohydrate-rich snack (see recipes for suggestions). Increased trytophan intake is often especially effective for depressed people who also crave carbohydrates.

The amino acid **tyrosine** may also help depression; it is often more effective in treating people aged forty and over. It is derived from the essential amino acid **phenylalanine**, which is present in most protein foods, and is converted in the body into its neurotransmitter derivatives, namely dopa, dopamine, noradrenaline and adrenaline. Dopa and dopamine act in the part of the brain known as the substantia nigra, and are depleted in Parkinson's disease. Low levels of brain noradrenaline and adrenaline have already been mentioned in association with depressive illness.

Pure tyrosine has been used successfully in treating depressed patients who suffer from a profound deficiency of brain noradrenaline. However, the way to increase your own tyrosine levels is by increasing your intake of phenylalanine. As mentioned in connection with tryptophan, eating a high protein meal will not increase the levels of tyrosine in your brain to the same extent as taking a supplement of the pure substance, but knowing which foods are phenylalanine-rich allows you to make sensible dietary choices that will help in the long run. There is also some evidence that small doses of tyrosine are more effective in increasing brain levels of neurotransmitters than large doses.

A high protein meal should be eaten, followed two hours later by a carbohydrate-rich snack to lower levels of competing amino acids. Protein foods with a high phenylalanine content include all those with a high tryptophan content, as well as almonds, lima beans, walnuts and chickpeas.

NB Some experts warn that neither tryptophan nor tyrosine (in the form of a nutritional supplement) should be taken at the same time as any of the group of drugs known as MAOIS – monoamine oxidase inhibitors – which includes Marplan, Nardil, and Marsilid. This warning has not been issued in connection with the dietary intake of naturally occurring tryptophan or phenylalanine. It is also worth noting that tryptophan has been shown to increase the antidepressant effects of the tricyclic antidepressant clomipramine (Anafranil), so there is every reason to eat tryptophan-rich foods if you have been prescribed this drug.

It is thought that a mildly excessive intake of the trace element vanadium may account for some cases of depression. Treatment with a low vanadium diet and vitamin C supplementation (as well as an extra measure known as chelation therapy to remove some of the body's vanadium) had beneficial effects on a number of depressed patients in one experiment. Vitamin C combats vanadium toxicity, and is, in addition, a potent anti-stress factor. If you want to reduce your intake of vanadium, try omitting fish and vegetable oil for three weeks and see whether your depression responds. Add extra vitamin C in the form of citrus fruits, tomatoes, cauliflower, potatoes and green leafy vegetables.

Depression in some people has been associated with a deficiency of **folic acid** (vitamin M). This is especially common in elderly, confused patients, and in sufferers from epilepsy. Elderly, senile people are frequently hospitalized, and this, combined with poor appetite, a largely cooked diet, and drug therapy may cause this vitamin deficiency which may then cause or worsen a tendency to depression and produce a snowball effect. People taking anticonvulsant drugs are at risk because folic acid depletion is a known side effect of many of these compounds. Others likely to need extra folic acid are heavy drinkers and anyone taking more than two grams of vitamin C daily. Aspirin also increases the need for folic acid.

A proven deficiency may have to be treated medically, but you can help to protect yourself against such a state developing by including folic acid-rich foods in your diet. Among them are dark green leafy vegetables, carrots, liver, egg yolk, whole wheat and rye flour, apricots, pumpkins and avocado pears.

A deficiency of **pyridoxine** (vitamin B 6) has also been associated with depression. Taking steroid hormones in the form of the Pill to control ovulation is associated with depressive mood changes in some women It has been suggested that the reason is that a relative pyridoxine deficiency caused by the oestrogen in the Pill, inhibits the manufacture of mood-controlling neurotransmitters. Treatment is by means of supplementary pyridoxine.

You can help yourself in this respect by eating food rich in this vitamin. These include brewer's yeast, wheat bran and wheat germ, black strap molasses, cabbage, canteloupe melon, eggs, beef and offal.

Recipes

Bearing in mind the importance of tryptophan to brain metabolism in depression, and the effects of competing amino acids, my suggestion is to alternate protein-rich meals that supply some tryptophan, and carbohydrate meals that help it to pass into the brain. Alternatively, you can combine protein and complex carbohydrates in the same meal, for a similar effect.

Breakfast Recipes

Start the day with a cup of herbal tea, or a glass of freshly squeezed fruit juice, instead of your usual brew. Lemon balm tea has an antidepressant effect, as well as a pleasant taste. Other herbs with a similar effect are lemon verbena and lemon thyme.

Lemon balm tea

While this can be conveniently bought in the form of tea bags from most health food shops selling herbal tisanes, many people enjoy making their own.

1 tbsp freshly picked lemon balm *or*
1 tsp dried herb
1 cup boiling water
thick slice of lemon

Bruise the fresh herb slightly with your fingertips, to help release its volatile oil. Place this, or the dried herb, into a small teapot, herbal infuser, or mug, pour over the boiling water and cover. Leave to infuse for about ten minutes, then strain (herbal infusers do this for you). Add your slice of lemon, and drink immediately. This can be sweetened by a small teaspoon of honey if necessary.

Calorie count: about 30, if sweetened with honey.

Fresh juice

Try this juice drink which is reputed to increase both energy and mental alertness. I have mentioned electric centrifuge juicers and you would need one of these to obtain juice from anything you cannot squeeze with an old-fashioned lemon squeezer. Some electrical supply shops sell them, and health magazines (e.g. *Here's Health*) frequently offer them for sale by mail order.

My juicer is made by 'Progress', and I can recommend it as sturdy and reliable. (The secret of cleaning the filter of particles of fibre is to hold it under the tap and rub it very gently with your finger tips or with a soft dish cloth.)

> several handfuls of spinach
> 4 – 5 carrots
> small head celery
> half large lemon

Wash spinach, trim and wash carrots and celery. Pass through juicer until you have obtained 4 fl.oz/100 ml of each type of juice. Squeeze lemon and mix all the juices. Take 4 fl oz/100 ml at breakfast time (when this juice is being prescribed as a form of natural therapy for depression, rather than as a useful juice drink, the recommendation is to take this quantity three times daily).

Calorie count: 40 to 50, depending on sugar content of vegetables.

Here are one or two 'general purpose' light breakfasts if you feel so low in the morning that you never bother with food at all.

Momento melon

This really can be prepared in a few moments, or the night before if you are always pushed for time in the morning.

> large slice of melon (about 6 oz/175 g)
> 2 tsp pumpkin seeds
> 15 fl oz/450 ml skimmed milk
> 1 tsp molasses

Scrape seeds from melon slice, and simply scatter with the pumkin seeds and eat at once. Stir the molasses into the milk, and drink. Alternatively, make a milk shake by scraping the flesh of the melon from the skin, and blending it with a couple of ice cubes, the molasses and as much milk as you need to bring it to the required consistency. Pour into a tall glass and scatter the pumpkin seeds on top.

Calorie count: about 250.

Egg energizer

This is another 'breakfast in a glass'.

> 10 fl oz/300 ml skimmed milk
> 2 eggs
> 1 dsp molasses
> 2 tsp sesame seeds

Blend the milk, eggs and the molasses with an ice cube. Scatter the seeds on top. If you prefer, toast the sesame seeds lightly. (You can keep toasted sesame seeds fresh in a screw-top jar.)

Calorie count: about 370.

Soya milk breakfast

Most health food shops sell cartons of soya milk, and half to three quarters of a pint/300 to 450 ml, chilled, must be one of the easiest breakfasts possible. Eat a piece of fresh or dried fruit with it, and/or some nuts, e.g. almonds, Brazils or walnuts.

You could even blend your soya milk with a little apricot purée (see below), or with a few ounces of canteloupe melon for a complete attack on morning miseries. It can also be substituted for skimmed milk in any of the recipes in this section.

Calorie Count: soya milk provides 240 calories per pint/600 ml.

Nut milk

If you are keen to try out the effects on your mood of tyrosine rather tryptophan, make a morning nut milk drink with either almonds or walnuts. Many people prefer almond milk as it has a sweeter, blander flavour. Use equivalent quantities of walnuts if you want to try them.

>30 fresh almonds
>8 fl oz/250 ml water
>lemon juice (to taste)

Remove almond skins by immersing in boiling water for 3 to 4 minutes, then rubbing them gently between finger and thumb. Soak in the cup of cold water for 2 to 3 hours, remove and dry them, retaining the water. Pound the nuts in a mortar or small bowl until they are finely powdered, then stir them back into the soak water. Strain into a small jug or glass, and squeeze the final drops out through a muslin cloth. Add a little lemon juice to taste, if you like.

Calorie count: about 160.

Apricot Astarte

The goddess Astarte is said to have been very partial to apricots. Dried apricots can be used in place of the fresh fruit.

> 4 oz/100 g apricots
> water to cover
> honey to sweeten
> 1 tsp wheat germ

Place fruit in a small saucepan and just cover with water. Poach the fruit over a low heat until they are soft. Remove the stones, if using fresh fruit, and place apricots in blender, adding just enough of the cooking water to give the purée a thick, creamy consistency. Sweeten to taste with the honey, and chill well. Serve with the wheatgerm scattered on top, or mixed into the purée. (If using dried fruit, soak them for a few hours in water to cover, and poach them in this.)

Calorie count: about 250 using dried fruit, and 180 using fresh.

If you are a carbohydrate craver, and have to have something more substantial in the mornings, try the following muesli which provides a good range of depression-fighting nutrients.

Moody muesli, mark 1

I have designed several versions of 'moody muesli', to help overcome several different unwanted moods. The tryptophan and carbohydrate content of this is designed to ward off depression. Substituting walnuts and/or almonds for the peanuts and Brazil nuts would provide more phenylalanine than tryptophan.

>1 tbsp wheat flakes
>2 tsp wheat germ
>2 tsp wheat bran
>1 tbsp Brazil nuts (chopped) or unsalted peanuts
>3 or 4 dried (or fresh) apricots, chopped
>1 tsp sultanas, raisins or currants
>1 tsp pumpkin seeds
>1 tsp molasses or honey (if required)
>juice of 2 oranges

Mix all the ingredients together the night before, and add a little mineral water to moisten them if the orange juice is inadequate. Eat the following morning with further fresh fruit juice if needed, or a little skimmed milk or low fat live yoghourt.

Calorie count: about 480 without the milk or yoghourt.

Easy protein breakfasts to help combat depression can make further use of the ubiquitous egg, or a portion of smoked haddock or cod if you are a fish lover. Try a lightly boiled egg with a warm roll or fingers of lightly toasted wholemeal bread, plus a scraping of margarine if you wish. If you prefer scrambled eggs on toast, cook the eggs gently over a low heat with a small knob of margarine, and a little skimmed milk.

Wholewheat and pumpkin seed bread

If you enjoy bread making, here is a nice easy recipe for wholewheat bread which I have adapted to provide extra protein, in particular tryptophan, which the seeds and soya flour provide.

>1½ tbsp brown sugar
>½ oz/15 g yeast
>16 fl oz/475 ml tepid water
>1¼ lb/500 g organic wholewheat flour

4 oz/100 g soya flour
2 tsp salt
1 tbsp clear honey
2 tbsp pumpkin seeds

Mix half the sugar, the yeast and 2 tablespoons of tepid water to a paste and set aside in a warm place until it froths (about 20 minutes). Put the flours and salt into a large warm mixing bowl, and the yeast mixture, the rest of the tepid water and sugar, and the honey. Mix to a smooth dough, add the seeds, and knead until smooth and elastic (10 to 12 minutes). Set in a warm place (e.g. airing cupboard), until the dough has doubled its volume (just over an hour).

Knead the dough for a further 10 minutes on a lightly floured surface, shape into a loaf and place in a well greased 2 lb/1 kg loaf tin. If you are making rolls, divide the dough into ten equal pieces, shape with your hands into ovals or crescents, and place on a greased baking tray. Put the bread back in the warm place for another half hour, and allow to rise again.

Place in a preheated oven (230°C/450°F or gas mark 8) and reduce the temperature after 15 minutes to 220°C/425°F or gas mark 7). Loaves take 40 to 45 minutes, and rolls, 15 to 20 minutes. Remove from the oven, and rap the bottom of the bread with your knuckles – it is done if it sounds hollow. If it does not sound hollow, put it back for a few minutes. Cool loaf or rolls on a wire rack.

Calorie count: 2755 for the whole loaf; about 160 per slice; about 275 for 1 roll.

Lunch

Ideas for packed lunches can include fresh fruit, salads, yoghourt, tofu (soya bean curd), cottage cheese and eggs (remember to eat only three to four eggs weekly), slices of cold chicken or turkey, prawns, shrimps and other seafood. Cockles, mussels, winkles and whelks are delicious and nutritious, but buy them fresh and eat them the same day – those packed in brine or acetic acid solution taste only of salt or white vinegar.

Whether you choose to include bread, rolls, biscuits, etc. depends on how much carbohydrate you normally eat and whether it makes you sleepy if you eat it for lunch. Including a little cooked brown rice, or some pulses or grains instead of bread, is one way of making a salad more filling without the need for bread. They also provide some carbohydrate which helps tryptophan or phenylalanine to cross the blood-brain barrier. Either eat a mixture of grains and pulses, or one of these with a few nuts, to ensure that you get the full complement of essential amino acids.

Salads

The quickest way is to wash and prepare the raw vegetables the night before and leave them lightly covered in the fridge. Pulses (dried beans, lentils, peas etc.) can be soaked all day while you are out or busy, and cooked while you are preparing dinner.

Alternatively, they can cook slowly all day in a 'slow cooker' (follow manufacturer's instructions). If you only remember them shortly before wanting to cook them, you can place them in a pan of boiling water, continue boiling for three minutes, then remove from heat, cover them, and leave them to stand for an hour. Cook as usual when needed.

Pulses and grains can be cooked in a larger quantity than indicated in the recipes, and will do several 'salad days' with different dressings.

How to cook pulses and grains

The best guide you can buy to the wide range of beans and pulses available in the shops is undoubtedly Rose Elliot's *The Bean Book* (Fontana). The author provides cooking times for all the pulses mentioned, as well as many ingenious (and delectable) ways of using them. As a general rule, all pulses benefit from soaking (see above) although this is not strictly necessary with lentils or mung beans.

Cooking pulses simply means bringing them to the boil, and allowing them to simmer until soft. I cover them with an inch and a half to two inches of water, and watch periodically to make sure they are not boiling dry. A teaspoon of cooking oil helps to prevent them from boiling over.

Both pulses and grains are tastier if you cook them in vegetable stock, which must be unsalted since the presence of salt prevents the pulses from softening satisfactorily. I use Friggs vegetable stock cubes available from health food shops, or the water in which vegetables have been boiled or steamed. If you have neither, a sliced onion, a carrot, a handful of celery leaves or a few herbs lend extra flavour.

Grains are also becoming more popular. If you are not already familiar with them, I can recommend barley, wheat berries (whole unrefined wheat grains), bulgar wheat (cracked wholewheat berries which have been hulled, steamed and roasted), buckwheat, and of course brown rice.

Grains taste better when fried very lightly before they are cooked – simply heat a teaspoonful of cooking oil and stir the grains round in it to coat them. They turn brown when ready (a few seconds) and the water or other cooking liquid can then be added. Like pulses, each type of grain is first boiled and then simmered – I give the cooking times of all those mentioned in the various recipes. Remember to rinse grains and pulses in cold water before cooking, and to pick them over for tiny pebbles and grit.

In addition to grains and pulses, salads should contain as wide a variety of fresh vegetables, fruit, nuts and seeds as possible. Here are some ideas to help you along. All can be prepared in minutes, and transported in plastic sandwich containers if necessary.

Lima bean salad

Lima beans are like butter beans, and the latter can be substituted for them if you cannot find them in the shops. Add a handful of walnuts, though, if you do use the butter beans, as they contain far less phenylalanine than lima beans.

3 oz/75g lima beans
6 spring onions
2 carrots
quarter of small white cabbage
cider vinegar dressing (see below)
1 dsp pumpkin seeds

Cook beans, cool them and place in bowl, with chopped spring onion and grated raw carrot. Mix well, moisten with dressing, and scatter seeds on top.

Calorie count: about 250.

Cider vinegar dressing

>3 tbsp cider vinegar
>1 tbsp runny honey
>small pinch salt
>black pepper
>1 dsp chopped fresh herbs (mint, parsley, thyme) or pinch of dried herbs

Mix honey well into cider vinegar, season and stir in herbs.

Calorie count: about 80.

For another salad prepared with pulses, use chickpeas, rings of raw leek, a tin of artichoke hearts, some shredded Chinese cabbage and a sliced tomato.

Bulgar wheat, beetroot and greenery salad

Bulgar wheat is an excellent grain for use in salads, and is very quick to prepare, as it only requires soaking in one and a half times its own volume of boiling water for ten minutes.

>2 tbsp bulgar wheat
>4 spring onions
>half a medium cooked beetroot
>1 large tomato
>3 tbsp beanshoots
>large handful chopped parsley

cider vinegar dressing (see page 40)
12 toasted almonds

Prepared bulgar wheat as above. Chop spring onions, beetroot and tomato into chunks, and mix into the wheat together with the beanshoots and parsley. Moisten with cider vinegar dressing, and add the toasted almonds just before eating.

Calorie count: about 475 without dressing.

Tarragon rice salad

This moist, juicy salad is very refreshing, and goes particularly well with shrimps or shredded chicken breast.

2–3 oz/150–75 g brown rice
1 tbsp olive or safflower oil (approx)
1 tbsp juice from pickled walnuts
1 large tomato
2–3 sticks of celery
4–5 button mushrooms, wiped
3–4 pickled walnuts
1 tsp dried tarragon (or slightly more of fresh herb)
3 oz/175g peeled shrimps or prawns
salt
black pepper

Boil rice and strain – brown rice takes about 20 to 25 minutes to soften. Mix in enough oil and walnut juice to coat grains thoroughly. Chop tomato, celery and button mushrooms and halve the pickled walnuts, and add to the rice, together with the herb and the seafood. Season lightly with salt and add a good grinding of black pepper.

Calorie count: about 450.

Sandwiches

Both wholewheat flour and rye flour provide folic acid, and bread made from them is perfect for sandwiches, or to eat with your salad. Most people have favourite sandwich fillings which they concoct for themselves, but here are a few ideas for fillings that will provide mood-lightening nutrients.

You can, if you wish, use either a scraping of butter or vegetable margarine on the bread, but I find that skimmed milk cheese is an excellent substitute, whatever the sandwich filling.

1 peanut butter, with some very thin slices of cucumber and tomato and a scattering of pumpkin seeds.

2 silken tofu, mixed with unsalted peanuts and a few beanshoots (if you have not used tofu before, buy a small packet from your health food shop – it is generally kept in the cool cabinet. Drain it, and use either as it is, with a salad, or mixed with savoury or sweet ingredients in sandwiches).

3 cottage cheese, mixed with chopped fresh apricots, or dried apricots, soaked in tepid water for 3 hours and drained.

4 liver pâté (see page 71), mixed with a little finely chopped onion, and some slices of tomato.

5 shredded chicken breast, mixed with a little lemon-flavoured mayonnaise, and watercress.

6 a large slice of cold roast beef (no skin or fat), minced and mixed with two teaspoons of horseradish sauce, and chopped chicory leaves.

To drink – natural mineral water, skimmed milk, fresh fruit or vegetable juice. Carrot juice is highly nutritious, and quite delicious, being rich, creamy and naturally sweet. It is best prepared immediately before drinking, as it tends to darken in colour and separate out. However, it keeps quite well in a thermos flask, so it is possible to prepare it in the morning and take it to work. You can also buy it (and other vegetable juices) – try the Biotta brand from your health food shop.

Spicy lentil soup

Finally, cold winter weather makes something hot and filling at lunchtime especially welcome. Try this spicy soup, which can be made with minimum preparation, together with a hunk of homemade wholewheat bread or a sandwich, with some fresh fruit to follow.

> 1 large onion
> 1–2 cloves garlic, crushed
> 6 oz/175g split red lentils
> unsalted vegetable stock cube
> ½ tsp ground coriander or cumin

There is no need to fry the onion and garlic first. Chop them up, place in large saucepan together with the lentils and spice, and cover with boiling water in which you have dissolved the stock cube. Bring to the boil, then turn down the heat and simmer gently for about 15 minutes. Liquidize, add a little salt if required, and eat at once.

You can add a little skimmed milk to this, to increase its nutritional value, but do this after you have liquidized it, as blending milk soups at high speed sometimes makes them unacceptably foamy.

Calorie count: about 550 without the skimmed milk.

Pub Lunch

Pub lunches on weekdays are notorious for causing afternoon drowsiness, but it is quite possible to eat and drink enjoyably in a pub without having to put up with this after-effect. Sparkling mineral water is very fashionable at present, and if you're really badly affected by mental torpor when you drink at lunch time, I recommend a glass or two of mineral water with ice and lemon. It is far more sensible to wait until the evening to drink, if you have a busy afternoon ahead of you at work, and mandatory if you intend to drive.

If you decide to imbibe, try a low alcohol lager, or at the most a 'spritzer', which is sparkling mineral water and white wine, in equal measures.

Most pubs provide a reasonable selection of hot and cold dishes, and salads, open sandwiches, cold fish or meat, hard-boiled eggs, cheese and vegetables are ideal. If carbohydrates do make you drowsy, then avoid bread or potatoes, and select those salad ingredients that will fill you without providing too much starch. Good choices included sliced beetroot (ten out of ten for any pub or restaurant that sells the genuine, freshly cooked vegetable without drenching it in vinegar first!), tomatoes, large chunks of cucumber, coleslaw, and celery sticks.

Evening Meal

Here is a 'fish supper' with a difference – no batter, grease, bright yellow breadcrumbs of dubious origin, or newspaper to throw away afterwards!

Cod and prawn parcels

The combination of cod and prawns should appeal to all fish lovers. Prawns and shrimps sound like luxury foods and can be very expensive. But the price of frozen prawns differs greatly depending upon the brand, and you only need a few at a time for this recipe.

Fresh ones are luscious, and the prices tend to be high. However, both prawns and shrimps can often be bought quite cheaply at fishing ports, and in small takeaway quantities from mobile fish vendors (the type that sell those delicious little cartons of jellied eels!) Also, do not despise *brown* shrimps, frequently sold more cheaply than the more aristocratic pink ones. Personally, I find them tastier, and it doesn't take long to peel either prawns or shrimps once you have got the knack.

1 × 6 oz/175 g cod steak, fresh or thawed
1 tsp olive or safflower oil
3 or 4 spring onions, chopped *or*
1 thick slice large onion, finely chopped
1 oz/25 g peeled prawns or shrimps
large pinch of dried dill weed
freshly ground black pepper
2 tbsp white wine

Preheat the oven to moderately hot (190°C/375°F or gas mark 5). Brush cod all over with the oil, and place it on a large piece of cooking foil. Scatter onion on top, and place prawns or shrimps on the onion, together with the dill weed. Season with the black pepper, and gather up the sides of the foil so that you can add the wine without spilling it. Close the edges of the foil, and place your parcel on a baking tray in the oven. Cook for 20 to 25 minutes.

Calorie count: about 260.

This is nice with some plain boiled brown rice, and baked tomatoes, which can cook in the oven at the same time as the fish parcels.

Baked tomatoes

3 or 4 ripe tomatoes
1 tsp sweet basil
seasoning
butter or oil

Thinly slice the tomatoes, and lay in a shallow, greased dish (an enamel plate, or the lid of a Pyrex casserole dish, is ideal). Scatter half to one teaspoon of sweet basil over the tomatoes, and season with a very little salt and some freshly ground black pepper. Dribble one dessertspoon of olive oil over the surface, or dot the top with small flakes of butter, and place in oven.

Calorie count: about 180.

Junket

Junket makes a pleasant change from yoghourt, and is a good way of including milk in your diet if you don't like drinking it. Some people make successful junket with skimmed milk, but I have never had any success with it. Use full cream milk as a treat, and once you have located a chemist that sells rennet, pay him the respect he deserves! It is a pity that far fewer shops sell it nowadays than was once the case.

1 pint/600 ml milk
1 tsp rennet
1 tbsp soft brown sugar
1 tbsp chopped walnuts or grated carob

Very gently warm the milk to blood heat — this is when you can dip a finger into it and it feels neither hot nor cold. Remove from the heat, and stir in one level teaspoon of rennet and the sugar. Pour into a dish, and leave at room temperature to set. Decorate the top with the chopped walnuts or grated carob. This is a naturally sweet, healthy substitute for chocolate and cocoa, which it closely resembles. Serves two.

Calorie count: about 600.

Herby liver casserole

Many people seem to dislike offal, particularly liver, which is a pity as it supplies both tryptophan and phenylalanine as well as many other nutrients. Tough liver is certainly offputting, but it can be deliciously succulent if cooked slowly. It also makes tasty gravy.

8 oz/25 g lamb's liver, sliced
2 tbsp seasoned wholemeal flour
1 tbsp safflower oil

1 large chopped onion
1 × 14 oz/350 g can tomatoes
large pinch of dried marjoram

Preheat the oven to moderately hot (180°C/350°F or gas mark 4). Heat the oil in a flameproof casserole, and gently fry the chopped onion for 5 minutes. Meanwhile, coat the liver slices in the seasoned flour, and then add to the casserole. Stir in the tinned tomatoes and their juice, and the marjoram, and bring to the boil. Put the casserole in the oven and cook for 40 to 45 minutes. Serves two.

Calorie count: about 590.

Yoghourt surprise

A cool, fruity dessert is pleasant after this.

5 fl oz/150 ml apricot or other fruit purée
1 dsp brown sugar
5 fl oz/150 ml chilled plain yoghurt
1 egg white, stiffly whipped

Mix the sugar into the purée, and place in a dish. Give the yoghurt a stir, and fold the egg white into it. Spoon this on top of the purée and serve.

Calorie count: about 330.

Try the following vegetarian stir-fry which really does take only minutes to prepare.

Quick vegetarian stir-fry

Stir-fried vegetables should be crisp and chewy, never soft. This stir-fry is nice with some warm wholemeal bread or a little steamed or boiled brown rice, and a green side salad.

2 medium carrots
quarter to half a small cabbage
1 small onion
large handful of bean shoots
2 tomatoes
2 celery sticks
1 dsp olive oil
Soy sauce
large handful of lightly toasted almonds

Chop all the vegetables up into small pieces, heat the olive oil in a wok or large frying pan, and add the vegetables. Keep the temperature fairly high, and stir all the time with a wooden spatula, coating every piece of vegetable with the oil. This will take 4 to 5 minutes. Add a shaking of soy sauce at the last moment, as this mingles wonderfully with the liquid in the pan. Give it a final stir and dish the vegetables out on to a warm plate, and scatter the almonds on top. A tablespoon or two of tahini sauce (see below) goes very well with this.

Calorie count: about 610.

Tahini Sauce

Tahini is pulped sesame seeds. It looks a bit like pale peanut butter, and you can buy it in health food shops. It is used for making hoummous (the Greek dip or spread made with sesame paste and chick peas), and several other delicious sauces and dips combined with other ingredients.

To make tahini sauce for a stir-fry, put a couple of tablespoons of tahini in a dish, and add olive oil and fresh lemon juice until you have obtained the consistency and flavour that suits you (keep tasting as you go!) Finally, add some chopped garlic if you like it, and a little chopped parsley.

Calorie count: tahini sauce made with 2 oz/50 g tahini and 1 fl oz/25 ml oil provides about 575 calories.

Fresh orange and melon jelly

The first course is filling, so a light dessert is a pleasant way of completing the meal. Make this at lunch time, or the evening before you want to eat it.

1 oz/25 g gelatine
1 large orange
1 tbsp brown sugar
ice cubes
1 cup canteloupe melon chunks

Melt the gelatine in 5 fl oz/150 ml very hot water. Stir the gelatine until dissolved in the hot water and set aside. Chop up the orange, and place it with the sugar and ice cubes in a blender. Fill it with cold water to the 15 fl oz/450 ml level. Switch it on for half to three quarters of a minute and strain. Return to the goblet, add the dissolved gelatine and blend again for a few seconds. Rinse out a jelly mould, place the chopped melon in it, pour over the jelly and leave to set.

Calorie count: about 190.

Here is an idea for a dinner party menu which, by combining complex carbohydrate with some tryptophan-rich protein foods, should keep you – and your guests – relaxed and happy throughout the meal. All the recipes serve four people.

South American soup

12 oz/350 g shelled Brazil nuts
1½ oz/40 g margarine
1 onion, sliced
half a head of celery, chopped
1½ pints/900 ml unsalted stock
salt, white pepper

5 fl oz/150 ml evaporated milk or single cream
paprika

Grind the nuts in a nut mill, or in a blender. (Blenders are perfectly satisfactory for this purpose but it takes a bit of time to dig all the small fragments of nut out from the bottom, where they collect around the blades.) Melt the margarine in a saucepan, add the sliced onion and chopped celery, and cook gently until the fat is absorbed. Then add the nuts, the stock and a little salt and white pepper. Cover and simmer until tender – about one hour. Sieve the soup if you like, but try the consistency first in case you prefer it as it is. Add the cream or milk, reheat, and serve with a dusting of paprika and sesame toasts (see below).

Calorie count: 750 per portion.

Sesame toasts

Put thick slices of wholemeal bread (not too fresh or crumbly) under a hot grill until browned on both sides, then split them down the centre as for Melba toast. Spread each uncooked surface with a little soft margarine, and scatter sesame seeds liberally on top. Place these under the grill a few seconds before serving.

Calorie count: about 200 per slice.

Beany beef casserole

Try the following casserole. Marinating the steak in the red wine makes it extra tender, and the wine makes the gravy delicious. Soya beans take three to four hours to cook, so soak and cook them the day before you want to use them.

Incidentally, red hot chilli powder is known in certain parts of Central America to induce a sense of euphoric wellbeing, and many people consume it frequently, for that purpose. So use as much of it as you think you and your guests will enjoy, without going overboard!

2 lb/900g stewing steak
1 lb/450 g soya beans
1 heaped tbsp seasoned wholemeal flour
2 fl oz/50 ml safflower oil
1 large onion, chopped
1 level tsp chilli powder (or more to taste)
one large yellow pepper, with pith and seeds removed, chopped
8 oz/225 g mushrooms
1 × 14 oz/375g tin tomatoes

For the marinade
6 cloves
10 fl oz/300 ml good quality red wine
1 tbsp safflower oil
1 tbsp soy sauce
2 cloves of garlic, crushed.

The day before, trim every scrap of gristle and fat from meat and cut into 1 inch/2.5 cm cubes. Crush the clove heads to release their flavour, and add to the other marinade ingredients. Mix, and pour them over the meat. Leave overnight. Cook the soaked soya beans in unsalted stock, cool.

The next day, remove the cubes of meat from the marinade, pat them dry with kitchen paper, and coat them in seasoned flour. Heat the oil in a fireproof casserole. Fry the chopped onion for 5 to 6 minutes, add the chilli powder and chopped pepper and fry for a further 3 minutes.

Add the cubes of meat to the casserole, and stir them round to coat them evenly with the oil. Add the mushrooms and tomatoes, and the marinade liquid (discarding the cloves first). Add boiling water if the liquid level looks insufficient, cover the casserole and place in the oven preheated to warm (170°C/320°F gas mark 3). Cook for about 2 hours, adding the soya beans 45 minutes before the end of the cooking time.

Calorie count: about 1300 per serving.

Steamed courgettes, runner beans, peas and some plain boiled potatoes are nice with this casserole.

Floating clouds

The rich, flavourful casserole is well complemented by this creamy and delicate dessert.

> 1½ pints/900 ml full cream milk
> 1 vanilla pod
> 3 eggs, separated
> 5 oz/150 g soft brown sugar

Bring the milk to the boil with the vanilla pod, turn down and allow to simmer very gently. Beat two of the egg whites until stiff, then carefully add 4 oz/125 g of the sugar, and continue whipping until the meringue mixture is stiff and shiny. Remove the vanilla pod from the milk, turn up the heat until it is just below boiling, and gently slide tablespoons of the meringue mixture on top of the milk. It is easier to form smooth egg-shaped meringues on the milk surface if you moisten the spoon with water before scooping up the meringue mixture. Let the meringues poach for 10 to 12 minutes, or until set, then remove them carefully and set on one side, on a clean plate.

Measure 1 pint/600 ml of the hot milk, and strain it. Beat the egg yolks and remaining egg white with the rest of the sugar in a bowl, then pour the milk onto the egg mixture. Return to the saucepan and simmer gently (DO NOT ALLOW TO BOIL), stirring constantly with a wooden spoon until the egg custard is thick enough to coat the back of the spoon. Strain the custard into a shallow dish, and arrange the meringues on top.

Calorie count: 340 per serving.

Beat Your Stress

When we are subject to stress, physiological changes take place which are most suited to 'fight or flight' measures. This marshalling of the body's forces, however, is an essentially primitive mechanism designed to help us cope with physical danger. We share this response with other mammals whose lives, in their natural state, quite literally depend upon it.

Early man must have found the flight or fight reaction equally vital. Faced with a hairy mammoth, a hungry tiger or simply a hunting opponent, the instant ability to attack, defend, run or wrestle was undoubtedly a life saver. Today, however, most of the stress problems we encounter are of a subtler and less physical nature. Certainly, the instant shot of adrenaline our bloodstream receives when we do have to take sudden avoiding action on the roads, escape from a potential mugger or put up a good fight in a judo contest, is as essential a part of our survival equipment as it is to any hunter in the wilds. But in the main, our stress is more likely to be compounded by money worries, marital problems, our jobs, families and domestic lives.

Our nervous systems react, however, in just the same way to both emotional and 'real' physical stress. The level of adrenaline in our bloodstream is increased by up to three hundred times that of normal, our muscles tense, our pulse rises, and our stomachs tighten. We cannot use any of these physical changes actually to rid ourselves of the things that are threatening us, and we therefore experience anxiety, which is a very unpleasant sensation indeed.

Anxiety has both physical and emotional components. The bodily effects raise the heart beat and sometimes the blood pressure, and increase muscle tension. This can result in fatigue, insomnia, poor digestion, headaches and migraine attacks. Anxious people tend to be tense, irritable and occasionally given to outbursts of violent feeling. Their concentration is nearly always poor and their enjoyment of life minimal.

Stress factors *in themselves* are neither good nor bad; the harm results from how we handle them. Certain stress factors can have a beneficial effect if we let them. Job challenges, the setting and achievement of a personal goal in one's hobby or sport, competitions of wit, creativity, strength, endurance and courage, all provide outlets for pent-up anxiety if we let them. Even very negative experiences, such as divorce, bereavement and being made redundant, become less painful and stressful if we adopt a positive approach.

Regular outdoor exercise, can have very real benefits; pounding round the park three or four times weekly does a great deal more for adverse stress reactions than do tranquillizers, sleeping pills, antidepressant drugs and visits to a psychiatrist. As well as getting rid of inner tension and pent-up emotion, exercise encourages the body's muscles to develop in size. The greater the amount of lean muscle mass, the less devastating the effects of stress when extra nutritional demands are not being met. Learning to relax, too, can add years to your life, and make it sweeter in the living, too.

Stress usually affects the appetite in one of two ways. It either increases anxiety levels to the pitch at which food — usually carbohydrates — is sought for and consumed constantly. Alternatively, it takes away all desire for food, and comfort is found — if the personality so dictates — in alcohol, cigarettes, strong tea or coffee, tranquillizers and/or psychotheraphy. Psychotherapy can be an excellent aid in the circumstances, especially if it incorporates lessons in relaxation. However, while stress is maximal and the appetite minimal, serious changes can take place throughout the body.

Stress increases the body's requirements of all nutrients. If insufficient carbohydrate is being taken, the stored glucose in the muscles and liver is used as an energy source. The body then turns to its own fat stores and its muscle protein with a view to breaking these down to provide energy.

At the same time, the kidneys tends to conserve sodium rather than excreting it in the urine in the usual amounts; more sodium than usual can only be retained at the expense of the body's potassium stores, however. Extra potassium is therefore required to cope with stress, and so is extra calcium. Calcium is withdrawn from the bones during stressful periods, and this encourages the development of the condition osteoporosis, or 'bone thinning', associated with brittle bones that fracture easily.

Which Foods?

Our reaction to food in relation to mood is highly individual. Some people (carbohydrate cravers) become irritable and edgy when deprived of carbohydrate, whereas others are calmer and better able to cope. Caffeine tends to increase our susceptibility to stress, and can be associated with pronounced anxiety, tension, migraine headaches, and insomnia. But some coffee-and tea-drinkers feel no anxiety, and merely enjoy the stimulating effects of their beverages. They find that they think and react more swiftly, and keep a 'clear head' for longer periods of time.

Again, carbohydrate has different effects on men and women. Since men seem to experience a calming influence after eating it, as opposed to the drowsiness many women feel, many men may find that a breakfast based on wholegrain cereal or bread helps them combat anxiety and tension during the early part of the day. Since protein for breakfast tends to make both men and women over the age of forty feel tense and less calm, women of any age might be well advised to opt for fresh fruit and/or fruit juices as the first meal of the day. In this way, they would avoid both carbohydrate-induced drowsiness and protein-induced tension.

Women under forty, on the other hand, could well discover that a light protein breakfast bucks them up, and improves their morning concentration. For both sexes aged forty and over, a high carbohydrate lunch is probably best avoided when mental alacrity and powers of concentration are needed to be at their sharpest. In this chapter you will find recipes for several different types of breakfast and lunch. This allows for as much individual choice as possible.

It is important to make especially sure that a daily supply of the essential amino acids is being included in the diet since the body's demands for protein inevitably increase under stress. If you eat a high-raw diet, and obtain your necessary amino acids from plant protein, you may well feel better and more able to cope, more quickly, than if you eat a diet high in red meat.

Because of the beneficial effects tyrosine is believed to have on stressed people, make sure that you include foods rich in its naturally occurring precursor phenylalanine (see page 29), in connection with eating for depression. The same applies to tryptophan, because of its tranquillizing effects (see page 29).

Calcium supplements are recommended by many experts, especially where the stress level is high, as the body's extra demands for calcium during stress have to be met satisfactorily. Extra need for calcium arises in people who smoke and in those who eat a high protein diet, especially one that is high in red meat. During and after the menopause, women are especially in need of calcium, since a lowered oestrogen level encourages bone thinning (osteoporosis) – see page 177.

Whether or not you have been advised to take calcium supplements, though, it is a good idea to eat calcium-rich foods in adequate amounts. This measure helps to combat the adverse effects of stress on the body, including the inner feelings of tension and anxiety. Foods rich in calcium include milk and milk products, cheese, sardines, salmon, soya beans, peanuts, walnuts, sunflower seeds, dried beans and green vegetables.

Magnesium has been dubbed the 'anti-stress mineral'. It is necessary for calcium and for vitamin C metabolism, as well as that of phosphorus, sodium and potassium. It is essential, too, for nerve and muscle function, and helps in the conversion of blood glucose into energy, always in heavy demand under stressful conditions. It also aids in protection against depression, and it is worth remembering that a moderate to heavy consumption of alcohol increases the body's need for this element as, too, does taking synthetic oestrogen (e.g. in the Pill). Lemons and grapefruit are rich in magnesium, as are green leafy vegetables, nuts and seeds.

The increased need for **potassium** that stress causes, makes its daily inclusion in the diet vital. Many foods contain some potassium, but you should include citrus fruits, watercress, bananas, tomatoes and as many green leafy vegetables as you can, as well. Alcohol, sugar, coffee, and diuretic drugs (other than those such as triamterene (Dyazide) or amiloride (Moduretic) which guard against potassium loss) all increase the body's potassium requirements.

Zinc has a reputation for helping to combat certain types of depression, and also plays an important part in brain metabolism, especially in maintaining mental alertness. Steak and lamb contain zinc in good supply, as also do eggs, wheat germ, pumpkin seeds and brewer's yeast. Alcoholics and diabetics have an increased need for zinc as does anyone taking supplementary vitamin B6 (pyridoxine). The need also tends to be greater in a hot climate, as zinc is lost in perspiration. If you are taking a lot of food that is rich in zinc, then your need for vitamin A will be increased.

Other vitamins are also useful when you are chronically anxious and stressed. **Thiamine** (vitamin B1) helps to equalize and balance moods and emotions. Depressed people often find that it bucks them up, while anxiety-ridden people discover that it has a tranquillizing effect. Most vegetables, oatmeal, milk, peanuts and dried yeast supply thiamine.

Niacin (vitamin B3) is necessary for normal brain function and for the health of the nervous system throughout. It protects against migraine headaches and high blood pressure (both stress related conditions), and enhances the utilization of food, so increasing energy.

With adequate supplies of tryptophan, the body can manufacture its own niacin. Supplementary quantities can be obtained from whole wheat products, brewer's yeast, wheat germ, roasted peanuts and the white meat of poultry.

Pantothenic acid (vitamin B5) is a great tension reliever. It aids adrenal gland function, which is very useful when they are working at an increased rate. It also helps to combat fatigue, a very common symptom in stress conditions and chronic anxiety.

The body can make pantothenic acid by means of 'useful' intestinal bacteria. It is also provided by brewer's yeast, whole grains and wheat germ, offal, green vegetables and chicken.

Pyridoxine (vitamin B6) see page 197.

Vitamin C is vital for combatting stress, and is sometimes known as the 'antistress vitamin'. Remember to pay special attention to your intake if you smoke, live in a city (because of atmospheric pollution), take aspirin regularly or are on the Pill.

Blackcurrants and citrus fruit are the best known dietary sources of this vitamin. It is also present in considerable amounts in rosehips and acerola cherries, but neither of these is commonly included in the diet. Wine or syrups made from rosehips, however, are enjoyed by many people.

Green leafy vegetables are also rich in vitamin C, as also are potatoes, cauliflower and tomatoes.

Vitamin E helps the neurones throughout the brain to obtain their vital oxygen supply in adequate amounts. It also helps to relieve stress-caused fatigue.

Good sources are Brussels sprouts and broccoli, wheat germ, wholewheat cereals, spinach, eggs and vegetable oils.

Insomnia

There are a multiplicity of reasons for poor sleep. Many are environmental, and there is little advice one can profitably give other than that of removal of the noise source wherever possible, or the use of wax ear plugs when nothing can be done about it. Health problems such as chronic pain, itchy rashes etc. should be dealt with by a doctor. However, sufficient is known about sleep and diet, thanks to recent research, to make sleep improvement in many cases perfectly feasible by the right choice of bed time food.

A high carbohydrate snack has been shown in experiments to induce more restful sleep. This means that, in the subjects studied, the total amount of REM sleep throughout the night increased, and periods of light sleep and wakefulness were reduced. (REM sleep is 'rapid eye movement' sleep, and is the deepest variety of sleep we experience. It derives its name from the fact that the eyes jerk from side to side during it, and it is also the type of sleep during which dreaming occurs.)

Drs J. M. Porter and J. A. Horne, who conducted this sleep experiment at the Department of Human Sciences, Loughborough University of Technology, pointed out that the actual quantity of carbohydrate taken before retiring has to be quite considerable. These beneficial sleep effects resulted from a snack providing carbohydrates to the energy value of 2,184 calories (i.e. a glucose drink and fried potatoes). A (relatively) low carbohydrate snack (crispbread, butter and salad), providing carbohydrates to the value of 787 calories, had little effect upon the volunteers taking part.

These may seem very heavy, fattening snacks to have to consume in order to achieve a good night's rest. Other studies however, have shown that 'a well known malted milk drink' reduced restlessness in younger people, and reduced periods of night time wakefulness in older people.

Probably the best dietary strategy is to eat protein food around lunchtime or late afternoon, to make sure you have consumed a reasonable quantity of tryptophan, and to take a carbohydrate-rich snack or drink to bed with you. It has been suggested that mothers may be able to improve their infants' sleep quality by eating a carbohydrate-rich snack before breast feeding, thus increasing the tryptophan content of their milk.

Recipes

Because tryptophan has a calming effect, as well as an antidepressant one, and tyrosine is effective in combatting anxiety (see pages 28–29), you should remember to include both tryptophan and phenylalanine when choosing protein foods when you are stressed. The other nutrients that are especially useful to us when we are stressed, and the foods that contain them, are detailed on pages 55 to 58.

The irritability that so frequently accompanies excessive stress and depression should, like that associated with alcoholism, respond to a high carbohydrate and tryptophan diet. Insomnia has also been seen to respond to a raised level of trytophan in the brain, and I will be giving some ideas for late night snacks and drinks at the end of the present section.

Breakfast

Here are some breakfast recipes designed to make you feel calm and capable of coping with the day, rather than anxious, wretched and ratty.

Herbal tea

A good herbal tea with which to start the day, in place of tea or coffee, is chamomile. It soothes the nerves, without making you drowsy, and is made from the flowers of the fresh or dried herb, or from ready prepared teabags. The dried flowers and the teabags are both available from most health food shops. If you decide to make your own, follow the directions given for making lemon balm tea, page 31.

Home prepared herbal teas contain no calories, unless you add something to them, such as honey. One teaspoon of honey provides around 30 calories, so this applies to all the herbal drinks mentioned unless indicated otherwise.

St Clement's cocktail

This juice drink really stimulates the taste buds and starts the digestive juices flowing – providing yet another argument for not going without breakfast! Whether or not you sweeten it with honey depends entirely upon how sweet a tooth you have. But I advise starting off by adding as little honey as you can get away with, and gradually cutting down the amount.

This will help you gradually to need less added sugar generally, as time goes on, which is an excellent thing if hypoglycaemia happens to be one of the causes of your anxiety and irritability (see page 5).

> 1 grapefruit
> 2 or 3 large oranges
> 2 or 3 tangerines or satsumas
> 1 lemon
> honey to taste

Since all the fruits included are citrus, they can be squeezed on an old-fashioned lemon squeezer. If you use an electric juicer, peel the fruit, leaving a little of the pith intact as this is an excellent source of bioflavonoids. Chop the fruit roughly and feed into juicer as usual. Serve with ice cubes. Some people prefer this juice topped up with sparkling mineral water.

Calorie count: about 175 (205 with a teaspoon of honey).

Tomato sunrise

This unusual sounding combination is quite delectable. Use either freshly squeezed or carton (unsweetened) orange juice; you will almost certainly find it easier to use carton tomato juice. Tomato juice prepared on an electric juicer is surprisingly disappointing – it is usually very thick, and when diluted has little flavour. It is usually far cheaper to buy tomato juice ready prepared than to buy a pound of ripe tomatoes for juicing.

> 5 fl oz/150 ml unsweetened orange juice
> 5 fl oz/150 ml tomato juice
> a few fresh catnip leaves if available

Pour the two juices into a large tumbler, add some ice cubes, and scatter the catnip leaves on the top. (They aid relaxation.)

Calorie count: about 100.

Carrot and celery delice

The flavour of carrot juice simply cannot be overrated. It is a shame that drinking it is associated in some people's minds with crankiness. It is as nourishing as it is pleasing to the taste buds.

> 3 to 4 carrots
> 1 to 2 oranges
> 3 or 4 large celery sticks
> 1 lemon

It is sometimes impossible to give exact quantities when listing ingredients for a vegetable or fruit juice drink – so much depends upon size, amount of juice etc. The proportions of this drink are one part carrot juice, to six parts of orange juice (use unsweetened juice from a carton if you are in a hurry), to two parts of celery juice, plus the juice of one lemon. It is a well-known remedy for nervous strain, and naturopaths (practitioners of natural medicine) who prescribe it, suggest 4 fl oz/100 ml three times daily. I suggest 5 to 10 fluid ounces (125 to 250 ml) at breakfast time, and thenceforth as you feel like it.

Just mix the juices together thoroughly, add a couple of ice cubes and serve!

Calorie count: about 140.

Banana milk shake

This is a banana milk shake with a difference! Use soya milk for its high tryptophan and calcium content, wheat germ for the vitamins it provides, and bananas for their potassium.

2 small ripe bananas
15 fl oz/450 ml soya milk
2 tsp wheatgerm

Place the bananas in the blender with 2 or 3 ice cubes, add the milk and liquidize. Pour into a tall glass, and sprinkle the wheatgerm on the top.

Calorie count: 350.

The Egg energizer drink given on page 33 would also be suitable in cases of stress.

Citrus fruit compôte

It is difficult to overstress the importance of natural vitamin C and bioflavonoids when it comes to coping with chronic anxiety effectively. The following compôte can be prepared the evening before and left in the fridge for quick consumption in the morning. Follow it with a hunk of warm wholemeal bread, and a scraping of skimmed milk cheese, and complete your breakfast with a glass of skimmed or soya milk.

3 ripe oranges
1 grapefruit
3 oz/75 g seedless grapes
1 tbsp roasted peanuts or sunflower seeds

Cut open the oranges and grapefruit and scrape out the flesh into a small dish. Wash, drain and mix in the grapes, and scatter the roasted peanuts or sunflower seeds on top just before eating. Although the combination may seem surprising, the crunchy, roasted nuts provide a very pleasing contrast to the sharp, juicy citrus fruit. Sunflower seeds have a blander flavour, or you can use a mixture of the two.

Calorie count: 360 with peanuts, 370 with sunflower seeds.

Super-porridge

All porridge, when properly made, is super-food, considering the fibre, protein, vitamins and other nutrients it provides. I have called this version 'super-porridge' as it is especially adapted to the needs of active, overstressed people who 'live on their nerves' and have to function in top gear all day, every day.

1 pint/600 ml water
2½ oz/60 g medium oatmeal
half tsp salt
1 tbsp wheat germ
2 tbsp sunflower seeds
1 tbsp molasses
skimmed or soya milk as required

Boil the water in a non-stick saucepan, and then sprinkle the oatmeal on the surface. Whip-stir with a wooden or plastic fork until the liquid reboils, then turn down the heat, cover the pan, and cook gently for 10 to 12 minutes. Put in the salt, give the mixture a quick stir, and continue simmering very gently for a further 10 to 15 minutes.

Stir in the wheat germ and sunflower seeds, and place in a bowl. Dribble the molasses on the top, and add as much skimmed or soya milk as you require.

Calorie count: 545 excluding the milk.

Oatmeal and walnut muffins

In case you dislike porridge, you can get your daily share of oatmeal in the form of these muffins, which also include the nutrients in egg yolk, walnuts and skimmed milk. Make them at the weekend or one evening – they will stay fresh in a bread bin, or wrapped in cooking foil at the bottom of your fridge.

To make 12 muffins:

> 5 oz/150 g self-raising wholewheat flour
> 3 oz/75 g fine oatmeal
> 1 tsp baking powder
> 2 eggs, beaten
> 2 oz/50g margarine or butter, melted
> 5 fl oz/150 ml skimmed milk
> 3 oz/75 g walnuts
> small pinch salt

Preheat the oven to fairly hot (190°C/375°F or gas mark 5). Place the flour in a mixing bowl, and gradually beat in the other ingredients until you have produced a smooth, creamy batter. Grease a 12-space bun tray, spoon the batter into each space, and bake for 20 to 25 minutes (they are done when a skewer inserted into the centre of one comes out clean). Leave the muffins in their tins for 5 minutes to cool, then finish cooling on a wire rack.

Calorie count: about 155 per muffin.

Try one of these muffins, warmed for a few minutes in the oven and spread lightly with skimmed milk cheese. Add a piece of fruit and a glass of whole or skimmed milk, and you are unlikely to hanker after mid-morning junk snacks. Try a glass of nut milk made with Brazil nuts for a change. It is made the same way as almond or walnut milk (see pages 34–5).

Calorie count for Brazil nut milk is about 180, using an equivalent weight of the nuts.

Moody muesli, mark 2

This version of muesli is made in exactly the same way as the 'mark 1' version on page 35, with the following variation in ingredients:

2 tbsp porridge oats
2 tsp wheatgerm
1 tbsp chopped roasted almonds
1 banana, sliced
1 grated apple
2 oranges, peeled and cut into segments
1 dsp raisins, currants or sultanas

Calorie count: about 520, without added milk or yoghurt.

Fish cakes

In case you are a determined 'cooked breakfast' eater, and feel that you *have* to start the day off with some protein even if it does make you feel tense, here is a recipe for fish cakes that combines both protein and carbohydrate, which should hopefully modify some of the anxiety-making effects of the protein content. They are equally good served either hot or cold, and therefore convenient for a packed lunch to eat with salad.

8 oz/225 g cooked or tinned fish
8 oz/225 g mashed potato
1 tbsp melted margarine
pepper
few drops of anchovy essence (optional)
1 beaten egg

wholewheat breadcrumbs
olive or safflower oil for cooking
small bunch of watercress

The best fish to choose would be either salmon or sardines. They are both rich in calcium, tasty enough to give your fish cakes a good flavour, and neither requires cooking if you use the canned variety. If you dislike them, then try kipper, smoked cod, or just plain cod. Both the cooked cod and the potatoes can be saved from an evening meal.

Flake the fish, and mix it in to the mashed potato together with the margarine, pepper, anchovy essence (if you are using a bland fish; sardines and kippers do not need it), and sufficient beaten egg to bind everything together. Shape the mixture into six round, flat cakes, brush with leftover beaten egg, and coat with the breadcrumbs.

Normally these would be fried in plenty of oil or fat, but they can be cooked just as satisfactorily with one teaspoon of oil apiece, if you fry them individually. Place a teaspoon of oil in the centre of your nonstick frying pan, spread it out with the back of a teaspoon so that it covers an area slightly larger than one of your fish cakes, and heat it until very hot. Place a fish cake in the oil, and turn the heat down very slightly, shifting the fish cake about now and then to stop it burning. Turn it over and cook the other side just long enough for it to brown slightly. Remove fish cake, keep warm and repeat with the rest of them. Eat with the watercress.

Calorie count: about 170 per cake using tinned salmon, about 135 using fresh or smoked cod.

Lunch

Use cold, cooked grains and pulses as suggested in the recipes in the previous chapter. Make sure that the fresh vegetables you use in your salads include a wide range of fresh, green leafy vegetables for the vitamin C, pantothenic acid, magnesium, potassium and calcium they provide. Good quality citrus fruit is available throughout the year in the shops, and you should try to make use of it at every opportunity, not only for breakfast and in the form of juice drinks, but also in salads, desserts and cooked meals. The following recipes will give you some hints, and you will be able to think of many more.

Chick pea and spinach salad

Chick peas make a salad into a satisfying meal or snack, providing both complex carbohydrates and phenylalanine. They take between an hour and an hour and a half to cook (see pages 38–39), and are often served with a garlicky mayonnaise (aioli) or other strong flavoured dressing as they have quite a bland, nutty flavour. Here, I am combining them with fresh, raw spinach which provides vitamin E and iron in addition to the nutrients mentioned above, and a simple lemony dressing to give added piquancy. Try it with a hard-boiled egg, a fish cake (see above), or some cottage cheese. A tangerine or satsuma rounds the meal off nicely.

3 oz/75 g chick peas (cooked)
4–5 oz/100–150g fresh spinach leaves
3 or 4 spring onions
1 large celery stick
2 medium tomatoes
half small raw beetroot, grated
1 handful mustard and cress, alfalfa or other sprouted seeds
lemon, honey and herb dressing (see page 68)

Place the chick peas in a bowl. Shred the washed spinach leaves, removing the stalks first if you wish. Chop the spring onions and celery into medium sized segments, and the tomatoes into small pieces to allow as much juice as possible to flow. Add these to the chick peas, together with the grated beetroot. Scatter the mustard and cress on top, and mix in the dressing.

Calorie count: about 350.

Lemon, honey and herb dressing

juice of 2 lemons
1 dsp clear honey
little salt and white pepper
a few mint and thyme leaves, shredded or
½ tsp of each of these herbs, dried.

Mix honey well into lemon juice, season, and stir in the herbs. Both mint and thyme have a calming effect.

Calorie count: about 65.

Another very pleasant pulse salad can be made by combining cooked soya beans with cooked (or canned and drained) red kidney beans in equal quantities, and adding a handful of black olives, some whole green beans, some rings of a large sweet Spanish onion and the segments and juice of a large orange. Mix in 1 oz/25 g of unsalted peanuts for added crunchiness (and tryptophan!). Dress with extra fresh orange juice, a little salt and plenty of freshly ground black pepper. Again, hard-boiled eggs go with this salad, as do tinned or fresh salmon, prawns, shrimps, mussels or whelks, or skimmed milk cheese.

Buckwheat, radicchio and celeriac salad

I would recommend a tasty but not too pungent cheese with this salad, such as Camembert or Brie. A medium strong Cheddar or some Gruyère are also good choices but remember their high fat content. Eat with a slice or two of wholewheat and pumpkin seeds bread (pages 36–7).

2 oz/50 g buckwheat
2 oz/50 g grated celeriac
5 or 6 radicchio leaves, shredded
2 medium tomatoes
6 spring onions

small orange, sliced
1 tbsp sunflower seeds

Cook buckwheat in unsalted stock (it takes about 20 minutes to soften). Strain and cool, and mix all the ingredients together. Dress with a squeeze of fresh lemon juice.

Calorie count: about 300.

Pasta salad with anchovies

Anchovies are just the thing to enliven the flavour of a salad based on cold cooked pasta, which can be a little bland without the right accompaniments. The wholewheat flour from which the pasta is made provides vitamin E, as well as zinc, some of the B vitamins, and folic acid. A hard-boiled egg goes well with this if you want to add extra protein.

2 oz/50 g wholewheat pasta
1 large tomato
3-inch/7.5-cm length of cucumber
a few radishes
half a red, green or yellow pepper
half a tin of anchovies, drained of excess oil
medium sized handful of watercress
a little black pepper
red wine and caper vinaigrette dressing (see below)

Cook and drain the pasta. Rinse well under hot tap and drain again to remove any suspicion of powdery deposit. Chop up the tomato and cucumber, halve the radishes, and cut the pepper into thin strips. Add to pasta. Mix the anchovies into the salad, and add the shredded watercress just before serving with a grating of fresh black pepper. Dress with red wine and caper vinaigrette dressing.

Calorie count: about 150.

Red wine and caper vinaigrette dressing

3 tbsp olive or safflower oil
1 red wine vinegar
little salt and pepper
1 tbsp capers plus a little juice

Mix oil and vinegar well together, or blend in liquidizer. Season and stir in the capers with a little of their pickling juice.

Calorie count: about 320.

Fresh fruit (especially citrus fruit, apples, pears, soft summer fruit, and cherries) is a very good way to round off this salad meal. Drink some natural mineral water, or a glass of freshly squeezed orange or grapefruit juice with it.

Sandwiches

Butter the bread thinly with skimmed milk cheese, a little butter, or vegetable margarine.

1 mix a couple of tablespoons of cottage cheese with a small teaspoon of yeast extract, some sunflower or pumpkin seeds, and a little chopped lettuce.

2 if you really must indulge a sweet tooth for once, make an open sandwich of a slice of wholemeal bread, topped with a heaped tablespoon of tahini, mixed with or topped by a dessertspoon of clear honey.

3 home made fish paste. Choose trout or cod, or some smoked haddock. Boil or steam lightly 4 oz/100 g fish (you can use a piece left over from a cooked meal), and remove any bones and skin. Place in a small bowl, and mash very well, adding a tablespoon of melted butter or vegetable margarine, and mixing thoroughly. Add a few drops of anchovy essence if you are using a mild flavoured fish, and season with nutmeg to taste. Use as sandwich filling with cress or watercress.

4 mash a large banana with a teaspoon or two of molasses, one teaspoon of wheatgerm, and three or four finely chopped walnuts.

5 buy a few fresh, juicy prawns, dress them with a squeeze of fresh lemon juice and a very little cayenne pepper and eat them as an open sandwich on either rye or wholemeal bread.

6 both liver and kidneys make delicious pâté, although one only seems to find recipes for the former. Both types of offal are rich in tryptophan, so eating either as a sandwich filling with wholemeal or rye bread should have a calming and relaxing effect when stress conditions prevail.

Liver or kidney pâté

This pâté is rich, as it contains a large amount of fat. Most recipes suggest butter, but I am substituting vegetable margarine, and if you buy a good brand, no one will know the difference once you have added the brandy and garlic. Use sparingly, though.

6 oz/175 g vegetable margarine
2 medium onions, chopped finely
1 large clove of garlic, chopped
1 lb/500 g lamb's liver or kidney, thinly sliced
salt and white pepper
pinch of sage
1 tbsp brandy

Melt 5 oz/150 g of margarine, fry the onion and garlic for 5 to 10 minutes, then add the liver or kidney slices, and fry very slowly for a further 5 minutes. Add the salt, pepper and sage, cook – still slowly – for a further three to four minutes, then remove from the heat and cool. Purée in a blender.

Melt the final ounce (25 g) of margarine and mix this with the brandy, then add both to the pâté mixture. Give the mixture a final blend for a few seconds, then remove and pack into a pretty ceramic pâté dish. Cover and place in refrigerator, where it will keep fresh for up to a week.

This is also a suitable starter course to serve at dinner parties.

Relaxation broth

The real name of this recipe is 'potassium broth', but I think that gives a false 'medicinal' name to a soup which is easy to prepare and very pleasant to drink. It appears in Bridget Amies' *Fruit and Vegetable Juices*. (Academy Publications Ltd.) and the author recommends it as 'strongly alkaline and eliminative, and useful in its relaxing properties for all cases of nervous tension . . .' Try it at lunch time, when you need to keep your wits about you all afternoon, yet stay calm, relaxed and tranquil.

1 cup finely grated cabbage
1 cup finely grated carrot
1 tbsp parsley, including the stalks
half cup shredded spinach
2 pints/1.25 litres cold water

Put the vegetables into the cold water and bring to simmering point. Keep at this heat for five minutes. The author then suggests that the liquid be cooled, strained and squeezed through muslin, but in fact if you simmer it for another five or ten minutes (less if you like your veg crunchy), and add a little low salt vegetable extract, it is even more delicious and far more filling.

Eat it for lunch with one or two oatmeal and walnut muffins, a piece of Edam or Gouda cheese, and a tangerine or orange.

Pub Lunch

The advice about pub lunches is the same as that given on page 43. If you tend to get especially irritable after day-time alcohol (many over-anxious people do), then there is even more reason for you not to drink at lunch time. Choose a fruit or vegetable juice with a high potassium content (orange, grapefruit and tomato all fit this category), and top up your calcium with a low fat cheese salad, some cold fish, and some cold cooked beans.

If you are unlucky enough to find one of those 'hopeless and helpless' pubs that can offer nothing beyond reheated commercial steak and kidney pie, or a beefburger in a bap (the type of place that has tomato sauce bottles on all the tables), then at least you can lunch upon a packet or two of roasted peanuts to supply yourself with extra tryptophan, and a bottle of fruit juice, and look forward to a more substantial evening meal.

Evening Meal

Here is a very easy and quick fish recipe for the evening meal, which should help you to unwind at the end of the day. I have adapted it from a recipe of the same name that appears in the *1000 Recipe Cook Book* edited by Isabelle Barrett and Jane Harrop (Octopus Books Ltd., 1976). It is supposed to serve four, but most people to whom I have served it, have polished off the whole thing without any problem at all.

Salmon bake

8 oz/225 g can salmon, drained and flaked
8 fl oz/225 ml tomato sauce (see below)
half tsp Tabasco sauce
3 tbsp yoghourt
3 tbsp cream
pinch of salt
pepper
half tsp dried sage
1 large tomato, thinly sliced
1 oz/25 g Cheddar cheese, grated

Put the flaked salmon into a shallow, ovenproof dish. Mix tomato sauce, Tabasco, yoghourt, cream, salt and pepper and sage together, then pour over the salmon. You can either use low fat yoghourt and single or double cream, or substitute the two of them with six tablespoons of Greek strained yoghourt, which is thick and delicious without adding much in the way of fat or calories.

Arrange the tomato slices over the yoghourt mixture, and sprinkle the grated cheese on top. Bake for 15 to 20 minutes in a preheated moderately hot oven (180°C/350°F or gas mark 4) until the top is bubbling and brown.

For the tomato sauce I use the simplest possible procedure – drain a large can of tomatoes, liquidize the contents, saving the juice for use in another recipe or for drinking. This provides about the right amount of sauce for the recipe.

Calorie count: about 595, using Greek yoghourt as suggested.

A baked potato in its jacket with a teaspoon of sour cream or vegetable margarine in each half, is nice with salmon bake, together with some canned or fresh broad beans, or some steamed broccoli which is rich in vitamin E.

Orange pancakes

Here is a delicious recipe for orange pancakes, well worth the effort of making. It can also be dressed up on another occasion to serve at a dinner party.

4 oz/100 g wholewheat flour
½ tbsp baking powder
pinch of salt
1 tsp grated orange rind
1 egg beaten
½ pint/300 ml skimmed milk
1 oz/25 g butter or margarine
3 tbsp low-sugar orange marmalade

Place flour, baking powder salt and rind in a basin, make a well in the middle, stir in the beaten egg, then half the milk, and finally the rest of the milk to form a smooth batter. Beat well. Heat the fat in a frying pan, and when it starts to smoke, pour in enough batter to cover the pan thinly (2 to 4 tablespoons depending on the size of your frying pan).

Cook until underside is golden brown, which you can tell by flipping up an edge of the pancake with a wooden spatula and peering underneath. Turn over on to its reverse side – it really does not matter in the least if it breaks a little, it will taste the same – and then, still using the spatula or a fish slice, slide each pancake as you make it out on to a warm plate. Put a dessertspoon of warmed marmalade into the centre of each and serve. Makes about six pancakes.

Calorie count: about 140 per pancake, 180 with marmalade.

Some evenings, getting down to cooking seems to demand more energy than you can possibly raise. On such an occasion, turn to your freezer and select a large lamb chop to cook for each member of your household, rather than sending off for an ersatz 'sweet and sour, and a fried rice' from your nearest takeaway.

Simple lamb chops with sage

1 large lamb chop
a little safflower oil
small pinch of salt
half tsp dried sage

Turn the grill on high, to warm it up. Brush lean surfaces of chop with the oil, and rub in the salt. Sprinkle with the sage, and press it in to make most of it stick. Place chop on the grid in the pan so that excess fat drips through, and turn the grill down to slightly above medium after the first ten minutes. A large chop that started off frozen, may take up to an hour to cook thoroughly. Test it periodically by puncturing the lean part with a knife and seeing whether the flesh is still reddish or pink. Even better, remember to remove the chop from the freezer before leaving for work in the morning.

Eat the chop with some plain boiled potatoes (new King Edwards go especially well with the flavour of lamb), a little mustard, and two or three sliced raw tomatoes.

Calorie count: one average chump chop, grilled, is about 350 calories.

Rapid fruit salad

This is a healthful salad as most of the ingredients are fresh. It is also sweet and succulent, because of the fruit canned in its own juice. Eat this with some plain yoghourt, preferably the Greek strained variety, and one or two oatmeal macaroons (see below).

> 1 small can fruit in juice
> (strawberries, raspberries, apricots etc.)
> 1 apple, cored and chopped
> 1 pear, cored and chopped
> 1 banana, peeled and chopped
> 1 orange, peeled and segmented

Peel the orange over the dish to collect any juice that runs. Pour the canned fruit and its juice into a bowl, add the chopped fresh fruit and mix them gently with a spoon, coating all the fruit with the juices. Serves two.

Calorie count: (with canned strawberries), about 130 per serving.

Oatmeal macaroons

These only take a few minutes to bake. Make some at the weekend and store them for when you need something to supplement a quick dessert. They also make a good accompaniment to lunchtime fruit or yoghourt.

6 oz/175 g rolled oats
8 oz/225 g brown sugar
pinch salt
1 tsp baking powder
4 oz/100 g melted vegetable margarine
1 egg

Mix all the dry ingredients in a basin, add the melted fat followed by the beaten egg, and mix again thoroughly. Using two teaspoons, drop equal sized portions of the mixture on to a well greased baking tray, and bake in an oven preheated to 180°C/350°F or gas mark 4, until the macaroons are golden brown. Makes about 24.

Calorie count: about 110 each.

Here is a vegetarian curry that may not be authentically Indian but is very tasty, nevertheless. Just as important, it supplies many anxiety-fighting nutrients, and is simple to make. Do not worry about the last five ingredients if you do not have them to hand or cannot be bothered with them. And by all means use a good brand of ready-made curry powder if you prefer.

Vegetable curry

2 tbsp safflower oil
1 large onion
1 clove garlic
2 tsp curry powder or 1 tsp each of ground cumin, coriander, turmeric, garam masala with ½ tsp chilli powder
8 oz/225 g potatoes, peeled and chopped
2 or 3 carrots, chopped
1 large celery stick, chopped
3 or 4 courgettes
1 tbsp desiccated coconut

piece of lemon or orange peel
1 tbsp currants, sultanas or raisins
1 tbsp chopped dates
1 roughly chopped and cored apple
8 oz/225 g butter beans, soaked and precooked or canned
small tin tomatoes

Heat the oil in a large saucepan, fry the onion and garlic for a few minutes without browning, then add the curry powder or individual spices. Cook for a few minutes, stirring so that the spices release their flavour without burning. Then add the potatoes, carrots, celery and courgettes, together with the coconut, peel, dried fruit and apple if using. Cover with boiling water or vegetable stock. Cook for about half an hour, or until the potato chunks are soft, checking the amount of liquid from time to time, and adding more if necessary. Then add the cooked butter beans and tomatoes, and stir in well. Continue to cook for a further ten minutes, then serve.

This is nice with some plain boiled brown rice, some spinach or broccoli, and a little mango chutney. Serves two.

Calorie count: about 535 per portion without last five ingredients, and about 660 per portion with them.

Apple snow

This is deliciously light and sweet, and can be eaten either warm or cold, although most people seem to prefer it well chilled. If you are still hungry, eat an oatmeal macaroon or two as well.

1 large cooking apple
1 tbsp brown sugar
large piece of lemon peel
1 egg white
pinch of powdered cloves

Peel and core the apple, and place with a little water and the sugar and lemon peel in a small saucepan. Simmer until apple is soft, then remove the lemon peel and strain the apple, retaining the juice. Push the apple through the sieve with a wooden spoon, and add enough of the juice to moisten the apple pulp without wetting it too much. Whip the white of egg until stiff, and fold it gently into the apple, together with a little powdered clove. Chill.

Calorie count: about 110.

Here is a good dinner party menu to serve guests who you are anxious should get along with one another. The ingredients have been chosen to soothe jangled nerves, promote amiable chit chat (not too many in-depth monologues, though!), and enable all the guests to view you – and one another – through rosé-tinted spectacles!

Summer apricot soup

This cold fruit soup is unusual, attractive to look at, quite delectable, and high in folic acid and tryptophan.

1 lb/450 g fresh ripe apricots or 8 oz/225 g dried apricots
water to cover
about 1½ pints/900 ml Brazil nut milk (see page 34 for method using almonds – you will need about 1 lb/450 g of freshly shelled Brazil nuts and 1¾ pints/1 litre of water).
2 tsp clear honey
1 egg yolk
4 tbsp double cream

Soak dried apricots overnight. Prepare the nut milk and set aside. Using either the soaked fruit, or fresh apricots, make an apricot purée as described on page 35. Place the honey and egg yolk in a small basin over hot water and beat until it starts to thicken. Remove from the heat, cool for a minute or two and mix in the apricot purée. Place in a blender with the nut milk, and blend thoroughly. Chill very well.

To serve pour out the soup into four bowls, and swirl the slightly whipped double cream on top for a marble effect. Serves four.

Calorie count: about 450 per portion using dried apricots, and about 385 using fresh fruit.

Roast lamb with coriander

Coriander and lamb complement one another perfectly. Fortunately, although strongly flavoured, it does not clash with the classic accompaniment to roast lamb – mint sauce – which is fortunate since mint has a calming effect.

Make your own mint sauce if you possibly can: finely chop as many mint leaves as you can, working the bright green, aromatic result into a small cup of cider vinegar and adding clear honey to taste.

1 × 4 lb/2 kg leg of lamb

1 oz/25 g butter, cut into small pieces

1 tbsp crushed coriander seeds

salt and black pepper

Smear the butter all over the lamb, especially where there is no fat covering the lean. Rub in some salt and freshly ground black pepper. Make slits here and there in the skin, and insert the crushed coriander seeds, covering as wide an area of the joint as you can so that it is uniformly flavoured.

Place it in a hot oven preheated to 200°C/400°F or gas mark 6, and leave for 25 minutes. Then reduce the oven temperature to 170°C/325°F or gas mark 3, and roast for a further hour and forty minutes. Cool for three or four minutes and carve when ready. This is lovely with broccoli, courgettes and new peas, and some small, new, boiled potatoes very lightly brushed with melted butter. Serves six to eight.

Calorie count: 210 per 4 oz/100 g serving.

Rosé dessert

Finish the meal with this light, fruity dessert. You can make it with fruit canned in their own juice when the fresh fruit are not in season.

> one fresh peach
> 1 dsp fresh raspberries
> half a fresh guava
> 6 or 7 fresh strawberries
> 4 fl oz/100 ml approx. sweet rosé wine
> whipped cream for garnish

Slice peach into a tall glass, add the raspberries, then the sliced guava, and top with the strawberries. Pour rosé wine over the fruit to come about three quarters of the way up the glass. Chill for several hours before serving, with a little whipped cream. Serves one.

Calorie count: about 240 per portion.

Snacks For Insomniacs

Here are two or three ideas for helping anyone who is tense and anxious to get a good night's sleep. A number of herbs help to promote sleep. Chamomile (already mentioned earlier in this section) helps you to relax, and this alone is sufficient to enable some people to doze off.

Others include orange blossom, available as teabags, lime flowers (which you can sometimes buy dried in health food shops), and marjoram, which you may either grow, or have as a dried herb in your kitchen. Follow the directions I have given for making lemon balm tea on page 31.

Maurice Hanssen recommends cider vinegar to help induce sleep, in his book *Hanssen's Complete Cider Vinegar* (Thorsons).

He suggests half a tumblerful of warm water, into which has been stirred two teaspoons each of cider vinegar and honey. This is no doubt an acquired taste for many people, but I find the contrasting acidity and natural honey sweetness delicious.

Finally, since carbohydrate releases tryptophan into the brain, and oats are renowned for their nerve restoring properties, bed time snacks and drinks based on oats or oatmeal are doubly good. Many people find a glass of warm, skimmed milk sweetened with a very little molasses or clear honey, and an oatmeal and walnut muffin (page 64) or a couple of oatmeal macaroons (page 76), help them to sleep long and soundly.

Oatmeal posset has an equally beneficial effect. This recipe was given in the *Reader's Digest Farmhouse Cookery* book (1980) and is reproduced with their kind permission. A posset is a thickened milk drink curdled with ale or wine. The thickener here is oatmeal.

Oatmeal posset

1 pint/600 ml milk
2 tbsp oatmeal
¼ tsp salt
2 tsp sugar (I suggest brown)
¼ tsp grated nutmeg
1 tbsp brandy

Put the milk in a 2 pint (1.25 litre) saucepan and sprinkle in the oatmeal and salt. Heat quickly, stirring, until nearly boiling. Remove from the heat and leave to stand for ten minutes. Press the mixture through a sieve into a similar saucepan, add the sugar and nutmeg and re-heat until nearly boiling, stirring to prevent the mixture sticking to the pan. Remove from the heat, stir in the brandy, and serve at once. Serves two.

Calorie count: 330 per serving using whole milk, 245 per serving using skimmed.

Increase Your Mind Power

In this chapter I will be giving advice and recipes designed to increase brain power and learning ability generally, and also discussing hyperactivity in children. Although the problems of hyperactivity and less-than-optimal intellectual and learning faculties are different from one another, an obvious overlap exists, and an impaired ability to memorize and learn is common to both.

Intellectual Ability and Learning

Many slimmers who skip breakfast find that they can concentrate less well as the morning passes. A number of studies have related a reduced ability to cope with tasks such as mental arithmetic with skipping meals. This underlines the brain's need for a constant supply of fuel and other nutrients.

While the brain can obtain the glucose it requires from sugar and other refined sources, as we have seen, it is altogether far healthier for the glucose to be obtained from complex carbohydrates. These contain the vitamins (especially the B group) and minerals which the brain requires simultaneously to utilize the glucose as fuel. High-sugar junk foods can actually slow the brain down, since they will not provide these nutrients.

The timing of meals and kinds of food eaten, have marked effects on intellectual performance, and these vary in men and women, (see page 2). Clearly, if you are made to feel sleepy and lethargic by a carbohydrate-rich meal, and find your attention wandering, you are better off with protein or raw fruit and vegetables, fruit juices, salads etc. whenever it is vital that you stay really alert.

Also necessary for clear thinking and intellectual activity generally, are certain unsaturated fatty acids. One in particular demand is DHA (docosahexaenoic acid), found in oily fish such as herring, mackerel, sprats and whitebait. Others are cis-linoleic acid found in vegetable oils, and GLA.

The saturated fat cholesterol, intake of which we try to limit in our daily diet, is found in large quantities in the human brain. It works in conjunction with the natural emulsifier lecithin, also found in plenty in brain tissues, together with the B complex vitamins choline and inositol. Both these vitamins are vital to brain functioning. Choline enhances the activity of the neurotransmitter acetylcholine, believed to play an important role in memory function. Inositol appears to take part in a biochemical process involved in the formation of RNA (ribonucleic acid), which may be used to store recent memory traces in the brain.

The process of memory is both electrically and biochemically dependent. Without the proper nutrients the proteins cannot be manufactured or utilized by the neurones to maintain desirable mental function, including that of memory. Faulty memory and bizarre thought patterns may be evidence that the sufferer's biochemistry is inherently unbalanced, or that his diet does not supply the necessary nutrients.

Iron deficiency can adversely affect memory, alertness, the ability to concentrate, and learning ability, as well as delaying the development of understanding and reasoning powers. Some intellectual impairment can occur when levels of iron in the body are not low enough to warrant a diagnosis of iron deficiency anaemia (a common condition in women, especially those who menstruate).

Drs Brian and Roberta Morgan, authors of *Brain Food* (Michael Joseph, 1986), suggest that the basic problem might be that the synthesis of brain neurotransmitters is adversely affected by iron deficiency. An alternative explanation could be that, the lower the level of iron in the body, the greater our susceptibility to the effects of heavy metal contamination, especially lead and cadmium. Besides inhaling lead from the atmosphere, and coming across it in some paints, we absorb it from tinned foods. Lead is one of the ingredients of the material used to seal tins, and food left in tins once they have been opened, absorbs this element on exposure to the air.

High levels of cadmium are also known to affect learning ability. We absorb cadmium from water that has passed through galvanized pipes, refined flour, plants that have grown on cadmium-rich soil, many processed foods, cigarette smoke and certain plastics when we handle them.

Which Foods?

The fatty acid **DHA** is present in fish oil. Inexpensive oily fish such as sardines, mackerel, herrings, grilled with a light brushing of lemon juice, or fried in a non-stick frying pan smeared with a teaspoon of cold pressed vegetable oil, are a handy way of taking DHA and valuable protein as well.

Choline is present in calves' liver and oatmeal, as well as in egg yolk, heart, green leafy vegetables, yeast, wheat germ and lecithin. Nutritionists recommend taking the lecithin supplement phosphatidylcholine since it seems that between 30 and 60 grams of choline are required before the memory appreciably improves. However, good sources of lecithin include peanuts, soya beans, wheat germ, ham and roast veal.

The B vitamin **inositol** can be obtained from liver, brewer's yeast, blackstrap molasses, canteloupe melon, beef brains and heart, cabbage and dried lima beans. Iron is supplied by red meat, beef kidney, heart and liver, pig's liver, clams, egg yolks, oysters, dried peaches, nuts, beans, asparagus, molasses and oatmeal.

Hyperactivity

Children who are truly hyperactive are found to share the following characteristics. They tend to be excessively active. Their movements are generally poorly coordinated, and they are very accident prone. Their attention span for any activity is extremely limited. They are disturbed by the slightest distraction, and much of their behaviour is destructive and aggressive.

Many children are hyperactive from birth and some are even so while still in the womb. They are restless, fidgety babies who cry almost non-stop, and sleep between three and four hours in twenty-four. Typically, they are poor feeders, whether breast or bottle fed, and often suffer from asthma, hayfever or eczema. They are not comforted by being picked up, cuddled and nursed, and this makes the bonding between infant and mother vulnerable to disruption.

Hyperactive children are prone to cot rocking and head banging, and they are excitable and often in tears. Although some of them have a high IQ, many have learning difficulties. They are often slow in learning to speak and they perform less well in school than they should because their powers of concentration are so minimal. Besides the allergic conditions already mentioned, many hyperactive children also suffer from catarrh, and other respiratory disorders. They are often abnormally thirsty. Boys are more often affected than girls, in a ratio of about six to one.

Although the number of children actually diagnosed as hyperactive is small there has been a rapid increase over the past twenty-five years in the number of referrals to child guidance clinics. Even allowing for an expanding population and better diagnostic techniques and facilities, the figures show a vast increase in children's behaviour problems since the Second World War, and has led inevitably to increased delinquency and vandalism. Research has taken a long, hard look at the possible causes, and while there remains much conflicting opinion on the topic, a number of positive findings have been made. A high-junk diet which is nutritionally very poor and contains synthetic additives, is believed to play a role in this as also are the large number of chemicals in our air, soil and water from pollution and radioactive wastes.

Lead, for example, absorbed from the atmosphere, affects intelligence and can cause classifiable mental retardation and/or behavioural disturbances that have much in common with hyperactivity. Tartrazine, a widely used yellow food dye, also accentuates the symptoms.

Research carried out by the Hyperactive Childrens' Support Group in the UK, and other studies, have indicated that many hyperactive children may have a functional deficiency of essential fatty acids (EFAs) – either because they cannot metabolize dietary linoleic acid normally, or because they cannot absorb it, or because their need for it is greater.

Which Foods?

The diet the HCSG suggest is an adaptation of the Feingold diet, which rules out food additives and a number of naturally occurring substances such as salicylates (related to aspirin). About two thirds of the children studied by the HCSG have also been found to be zinc deficient, and although this mineral is generally given as a dietary supplement, foods rich in this mineral are also important (see page 199).

A further important supplement is evening primrose seed oil, as this and human breast milk are the only known sources of reasonable supplies of the EFA gammalinolenic acid (see page 19).

It is also thought that hyperactive behaviour in a number of children is related to a high sugar intake, as well as to caffeine (present in many fizzy bottled drinks). The wholefood diet recommended in this book excludes these as a matter of course.

The recipes given here will supply hyperactive children with the essential fatty acids and zinc of which they are short. But there is every reason for also including foods with a naturally tranquillizing influence and you will see I have included foods with a known calming effect, such as appeared in the section on anxiety. I have also included some wheat and cereal products, and milk, in some of the recipes. Although some hyperactive children are sensitive to these foods, not all are, and it is worth trying a simple elimination diet for a few days (see 'Food allergy' p. 7) to make certain.

I have also included as much protein as possible, since the stress upon mind and body of being hyperactive takes a huge toll of children's natural resources. This is sometimes – quite understandably – overlooked by parents and teachers who care for and teach after hyperactive children, so great is the stress upon themselves. In the present context of hyperactivity and poor learning, the dangers of both cadmium and lead toxicity should also be remembered, (see page 84), as well as the ill effects of sub-clinical iron deficiency.

Recipes

I have found it simplest to give recipes for half adult-sized helpings. These can be easily tailored to suit the needs of the individual child.

Breakfasts

Whatever you do avoid the following three mistakes. DON'T let a hyperactive child start the morning with a bottle of fizzy cola drink — the high sugar and caffeine content, not to mention the additives it contains, represent a recipe for disaster. DON'T let the child go without breakfast altogether — even if you're obliged to resort to frank bribery to get your own way. And DON'T tell him or her to eat or drink anything 'because it is good for them'. This is guaranteed to provoke mutiny!

Coffee and tea should also be ruled out because of their caffeine content. Whether children take to a herbal tea is a matter of luck — certainly the lemon balm tea for which the recipe is given on page 31 would be suitable. You could say the drink was a special lemon one and grate a little extra lemon peel into the tea before it infuses, as well as floating a lemon slice on the top.

Two herbs reputed to improve the power of memory, are sage and rosemary. Shakespeare's Ophelia gave Hamlet a rosemary sprig, saying: 'There's rosemary, that's for remembrance. Pray, love, remember' and Greek youths used to tuck a piece of this herb behind their ear when sitting for examinations, as its powers of aiding the recollection of facts were widely revered.

Maurice Messegué (who recommends rosemary for many ailments although not for a flagging memory) suggests making an infusion of fresh rosemary by pouring 1¾ pints (1 litre) of boiling water over half a handful of the flowering branches, and allow the tea to brew for 5 or 6 minutes. This is then strained and served. Add a little honey if you like.

Tea from the dried herb can be made in the same way as lemon balm tea, as also can sage.

Fresh juice

Most fresh fruit and vegetable juices are suitable for hyperactive children. If they have a sweet tooth, they will naturally tend to go for those with the highest sugar content, and apple, pear, orange, carrot and beetroot belong to this category.

The following is a pleasant mixture:

> one large eating apple
> one juicy pear
> 2 large carrots

Prepare fruit and feed into juicer. Pour juice into a glass, add some ice cubes, and provide two coloured drinking straws. A small saucer of pumpkin seeds might appeal to a child as unusual – most children like the nutty flavour. It is a good way of increasing their zinc intake.

Calorie count: about 80, depending on sugar content of fruit and carrots.

For increased mental alacrity, try the following juice combination which is high in iron, potassium and magnesium, as well as choline and vitamins C and E.

> 9 or 10 medium carrots
> handful of washed spinach leaves
> 2 celery sticks

Juice all the vegetables, mix well and drink at once. Apart from the nutrients it provides, the carrots and celery juice in this recipe acts as a pleasant tasting 'vehicle' for the spinach juice which some people find too bitter taken alone.

Calorie count: about 110, depending on sugar content.

Other breakfast recipes that would also suit children in half quantities include Momento melon (p. 33), Egg energizer (p. 33), Soya milk breakfast (p. 34) and Nut milk (p. 34). Apricot Astarte (p. 35) would also suit children and adults alike, but the following idea is even more suitable to the needs of hyperactive children and poor learners, as it provides iron as well as zinc.

Peach amazement

The name I have given this recipe is not undeserved. Dried peaches (the providers of iron in this case) are astonishingly dreary to look at – dried up, brownish bits that rarely attract the attention of anyone who has not tried them previously. Like peach brandy, dried peaches are far less widely available than their apricot counterpart, and enthusiasts frequently haunt health food shops in the hope that a packet may be lurking, overlooked, on one of the shelves.

4 oz/100 g dried peaches
water to cover
1 dsp pumpkin seeds or
1 dsp wheatgerm

Cover dried peaches with tepid water and soak for three or four hours. Poach the fruit over a low heat until they are soft, place in blender, and liquidize with a little of the juice until a creamy purée forms. Cool and serve in a tall glass with pumpkin seeds or wheatgerm sprinkled on top. Serve a glass of skimmed, soya or nut milk to drink. Alternatively, milk of any of these types can be added to the purée while still in the blender, together with a couple of ice cubes, and a milk shake made.

Dried peaches are quite sweet, but you can stir in a dessertspoon of molasses if you like, for extra iron and some vitamin B 6. Serves one adult, half this quantity for a child.

Calorie count: about 350 with ½ pint (300 ml) of skimmed milk, 400 with the molasses.

Porridge is another breakfast food that many children enjoy (see recipe, page 63). Oats are a natural tranquillizer, and also enhance good intellectual function because of the iron they supply.

Moody muesli, mark 3

This muesli is designed with hyperactive children in mind. It is equally suitable for the enhancement of brain power, and so suitable to non-hyperactive children too, and to adults wanting to start off the day with a clear, active mind. Just increase the quantities to suit your needs.

1 level dsp oatmeal, soaked overnight in fresh orange juice
1 tbsp chopped almonds, Brazil nuts, or unsalted peanuts
1 sweet, juicy eating apple
a little top of the milk
1 tsp clear honey

Mix the soaked oatmeal with the nuts; grate or finely chop the apple and stir it in. Add sufficient top of the milk to moisten to the required consistency, and drizzle the clear honey on top.

Calorie count: about 400.

For lovers of savoury foods (and this includes many children), fish and eggs are excellent choices. Both supply good protein and an excellent range of nutrients, of particular note in the present context being the essential fatty acid DHA (in oily fish), and zinc (in egg yolk).

Both adults and children are often happy to indulge in the old, favourite custom of dipping 'soldiers' into a lightly boiled egg yolk. Thin fingers of lightly buttered bread or toast are essential to this pastime, as is a 'properly' boiled egg. Four minutes is the usual length of time for the white of a medium sized egg to set, leaving the yolk deliciously runny, timed from the moment the egg is lowered into the gently boiling water.

Oatmeal bread

Here is a recipe for oatmeal bread, which is chewy in texture, and makes good toast. It is very pleasant with eggs however they are cooked. Some people like to scramble or poach eggs and place them on a slice of *untoasted* oatmeal bread, as they claim that the flavour of the oatmeal, which complements eggs so well, is more apparent in this form.

8 oz/225 g rolled oats or medium fine oatmeal
10 fl oz/300 ml warm milk

1 tsp honey
5 fl oz/150 ml warm water
2 tsp dried yeast
12 oz/350 g wholemeal flour
2½ level tsps salt
1 tbsp safflower oil

Place oatmeal in a bowl, pour over them the warm milk and leave for half an hour. Meanwhile, dissolve the honey in the warm water, sprinkle the yeast on top and set aside for ten minutes until it is frothy. Then mix together the flour and salt in a bowl, add the oil, the yeast liquid, and the oats. Mix well, turn out onto a floured board, and knead for ten minutes.

Wash the bowl, rub its inner surface lightly with oil, put back the dough, cover with oiled polythene and leave to rise in a warm place for about an hour, during which it will have doubled in size. Knead the dough again for around three minutes, divide into two pieces and shape into loaves, place in two well oiled or greased 1 lb/450 g loaf tins, cover with the polythene again and leave to rise again in a warm place for about 40 minutes. Pre-heat the oven to hot (200°C/400°F or gas mark 6) and bake for 30 minutes. Cool the loaves on a wire rack.

Although all the familiar 'oily' fish contain the precious ingredient DHA, the memory and intellect enhancer, few people are likely to want to face grilling herrings, or frying sprats and whitebait, at breakfast time. The best most of us can hope for is the chance to buy a genuine smoked kipper from a fishmonger, as opposed to the poor, dyed slithers of ersatz kipper to be found lurking in supermarket deep freezers.

Having obtained your kipper, 'jug' it for breakfast rather than frying it for supper. It will get your day off to a very good start, and the method is quick and odourless. Simply fill a conveniently sized jug with boiling water, immerse the kipper in it, tail end uppermost, and leave there for ten to fifteen minutes.

Kippered eggs

These are nice, and quite popular with children, hyperactive and otherwise. Eat them with a slice of oatmeal bread, spread lightly with vegetable margarine or skimmed milk cheese, and finish with a fresh orange and a glass of Brazil nut or skimmed milk.

> 1 small kipper
> 2 eggs
> 1 oz/25 g margarine
> salt and pepper
> nutmeg or powdered rosemary

Cook kipper as described above. Scramble eggs with the margarine and a little drop of skimmed milk if you like, and season. While still on the soft side, remove the pan from the stove, retrieve kipper from its jug, drain it, and flake it up, mixing it into the scrambled eggs. Season with a very little powdered rosemary or freshly grated nutmeg. Serves one adult.

Calorie count: about 267.

Here is a recipe that combines protein and carbohydrate, and provides some tryptophan into the bargain.

Cottage cheese on toast

> 1 slice oatmeal bread (see page 91)
> scraping of margarine
> 2 oz/50 g cottage cheese
> pepper
> few mandarin segments from canned fruit in water or juice
> small bunch of watercress

Toast the bread lightly, spread with the margarine and

spoon the cheese on top. Put under the grill until the cheese is warmed through and turning golden, then remove, add a little pepper and serve, decorated with mandarin segments and watercress.

Calorie count: 180

Lunch

The lunches based on salads, which have to be transported in individual polythene containers and eaten with a fork or spoon, are in the main more suitable for adults taking a packed lunch to work, than for school children who are more in need of simple, sustaining foods that can be eaten with their fingers. So I have planned most of the former with adults in mind, while giving ideas for sandwiches, soups, drinks and snacks that would suit both children and adults. They are of course interchangeable, to suit individual tastes and requirements.

Salad lunches

Cold, cooked pasta, grains and pulses, with a light dressing, go well with the protein foods and salad vegetables that provide memory-enhancing nutrients. Green, leafy vegetables are a good source of choline, cabbage in addition supplies inositol, and iron can be obtained from asparagus and spinach. The best types of protein foods to select include eggs, beef (especially the heart, kidneys and liver), pig's kidney, clams and oysters, and of course all the oily varieties of fish for their DHA content.

Millet and smoked oyster salad

There is still a tendency in this country to associate millet with birds, but for many people living in equatorial countries it is a staple grain. Two very good points in its favour are its high iron content, and the fact that it is quick and easy to cook. It also tastes good! It is, however, a trifle on the bland side, and when included as a main salad ingredient it is best combined with other foods that both mingle their flavour with its own, and complement its soft, rice-like consistency.

> 2 oz/50 g millet
> 2 medium tomatoes
> 6 or 7 spring onions
> handful of fresh parsley
> 1 tbsp pumpkin seeds
> small tin smoked oysters
> 3 or 4 fl oz/75 to 100 ml tomato juice
> Worcestershire sauce
> salt and pepper

Cook the millet (see 'How to cook pulses and grains', pages 38–9) – this takes 15 to 20 minutes. Drain and cool, then mix with chopped tomatoes and spring onions, finely chopped parsley, pumpkin seeds and the drained oysters. Moisten (without flooding) the salad with the tomato juice, to which you have added a few drops of Worcestershire sauce, and the salt and pepper, and mingle well. (You can use some carton tomato juice, or a little of the juice from a can of tomatoes).

Calorie count: about 280.

You can add extra protein to this salad if you wish, with a couple of hard-boiled eggs, chopped up and mixed in with the other ingredients. Eat your salad with a slice or two of oatmeal bread (page 91), and finish the meal with a banana or three or four dried peaches.

Flageolet salad with bean shoots and green beans

Flageolet beans are many people's favourite pulse. They have a particularly delicious flavour, which is strong enough to stand up to boiling in unflavoured water, although like other pulses they do benefit from the addition of unsalted stock or root vegetables to their cooking water.

All three of the beans used in this salad go well with garlic, but if you happen not to like it, use the vinaigrette dressing plain.

> 2 oz/50 g flageolet beans
> 2 tbsp green or runner beans, frozen or fresh
> handful of bean shoots
> 6 or 7 radishes
> 2 or 3 spring onions
> 1 tbsp chopped blanched almonds
> green garlicky dressing (see below)

Cook, drain and cool the flageolets and the green beans. Chop the latter in biggish lengths, and mix in with the flageolets, together with the bean shoots, sliced radishes, and spring onions. Mix in the salad dressing, and scatter the almonds on the top.

Calorie count: about 315.

Green garlicky dressing

> 3 tbsp olive oil
> 1 tbsp white wine vinegar
> 1 large garlic clove, finely chopped
> pinch brown sugar
> little salt and black pepper
> $1/3$ tsp mustard powder
> 2 tsp each finely chopped chives and parsley

Mix or blend all the ingredients together, and use as required.

Calorie count: about 420.

This salad goes well with tuna fish, a lightly buttered herb oatcake (see page 97), and a large tomato.

Herb oatcakes

8 oz/225 g fine oatmeal
half tsp baking powder
pinch salt
2 tbsp melted vegetable margarine
5 fl oz/150 ml boiling water
1 tsp dried sweet basil or marjoram

Mix the oatmeal, baking powder and salt, add the melted margarine and boiling water, mix well in and then add the herbs. Knead the dough lightly, form it into a ball when it is well amalgamated, and roll it out into a circle on a board sprinkled with oatmeal to stop it sticking (dust your hands with a little oatmeal or ordinary flour before kneading, too).

Cut into four, and cook in an ungreased frying pan over a low, steady heat until pale brown and cooked through (about 7 or 8 minutes per side). Remove and leave to cool on a wire rack.

Calorie count: about 310 per cake.

English salad

Most people mock the typical English salad as consisting of a couple of wilted lettuce leaves, a slice of cucumber, some vinegar-saturated beetroot out of a jar, and a squashy tomato. Here is a salad that is simplicity itself, and which makes use of the best of English garden produce in the height of the season.

half a small cos lettuce
6 spring onions
several slices of cucumber with the peel
2 or 3 baby tomatoes
a handful of mustard and cress
3 or 4 slices of fresh cooked beetroot

3 or 4 baby carrots, scrubbed but unpeeled
1 tbsp snipped chives

Simply wash all the vegetables, bought as fresh as possible or picked from your garden, dry on kitchen paper, and cut to a suitable size. All you need in the way of dressing is a very few drops of malt vinegar, a very little salt and a grinding of black pepper.

This is delicious eaten with hard-boiled eggs prepared as follows:

Pilchard eggs

These are similar in many ways to Scotch eggs, but use fish as the protein in the 'shell' instead of sausage meat.

2 eggs
4 oz/100 g tinned pilchards, drained and patted dry
1 tsp fresh sage, finely chopped or 1 tsp dried sage
finely grated rind of half a lemon
1/4 tsp freshly grated nutmeg
salt and a little black pepper
2 or 3 slices stale wholemeal bread, crumbed
1 beaten egg
safflower oil for frying

Boil the eggs and peel them. Set on one side. Put the carefully drained pilchards in a bowl with the sage, lemon rind and nutmeg, season with the salt and pepper and, using a wooden spoon or your fingers, work in enough wholemeal breadcrumbs to form a thick paste. Cover each egg with a coating of the fish mixture, dip the eggs in the beaten egg and press the rest of the crumbs over their surface to form an even coat.

Heat the oil in a frying pan and, when it is very hot and only just starting to smoke, fry the eggs in the oil until they turn a deep golden colour, turning them so that they cook evenly. Remove them from the pan with a draining spoon, allow them to cool slightly on absorbent paper, and halve them. Children love these, incidentally, and they are a popular 'find' in a school lunch box.

Sandwiches

Here are some ideas for sandwich fillings to appeal both to over-active children, and other members of the family anxious to eat in such a way that their 'brain power' receives the right nutrients for optimal activity. You can use wholemeal or oatmeal bread for these, or sandwich a couple of oatcakes together with the less moist fillings.

1 crunchy peanut butter, mixed with a little yeast extract, a teaspoon of wheatgerm and some pumpkin seeds.

2 cottage cheese, drained of whey, and mashed with grated walnuts and a few chopped prawns or shrimps.

3 smoked cod, cooked, drained and mashed with a little vegetable margarine, some nutmeg, and a teaspoon of roasted sesame seeds.

4 eggs, hard boiled for 5 to 6 minutes, mashed with finely chopped mustard and cress and a very little tomato pulp.

5 sardines, drained of oil or tomato sauce, and mixed with chopped watercress and sliced radishes.

6 finely shredded chicken breast, mixed with a couple of teaspoons of mayonnaise, a teaspoon of wheatgerm, and a hard-boiled egg yolk.

7 beef liver or kidney pâté (see page 71), with thin slices of tomato and cucumber.

8 low sugar jam or marmalade, mixed with grated Brazil nuts or almonds, and a teaspoon of wheat germ.

Children love to find surprise 'extras' in their lunch bags, so include a few Brazil nuts or lightly toasted almonds, a tablespoon of pumpkin seeds, a few dried apricots or peaches, or some unsalted peanuts, wrapped in individual 'screws' of greaseproof paper.

Broccoli soup

Green leafy vegetables are so rich in the vital brain nutrient, iron, that they really should be used in as many ways as possible. Try this soup, made from broccoli or calabrese. A slice or two of oatmeal bread is its perfect accompaniment.

1 medium onion, chopped
2 pints/1.25 l unsalted vegetable stock
1½ lb/675 g broccoli tops and small stalks
a little grated nutmeg
a little grated lemon rind and 1 tbsp lemon juice
salt and pepper
3 tbsp plain yoghurt

Although most soup recipes give strict instructions about frying the onion and other vegetables as a preliminary, it really is not mandatory. Not doing so saves you time and labour, and avoids the unnecessary use of oil or margarine.

Place the onion in a large saucepan, add the stock and bring to the boil. Cook for ten minutes, then add the broccoli (it is even quicker to save some cooked green vegetable from the previous evening meal). Add the nutmeg, lemon rind and juice, salt and pepper, bring to the boil again and turn down until it is simmering steadily. Cook for 20 to 30 minutes, until the vegetables are soft. Place in the blender, and liquidize for about one minute, then return to the saucepan, reheat, and stir in the yoghourt.

Calorie count: 380.

Most cake goes well with fresh fruit, and this one makes a pleasant accompaniment to a juicy pear, apple or orange.

Lunch cake

>6 oz/175 g wholemeal flour
>2 oz/50 g soya flour
>1 tsp mixed spice
>pinch of salt
>3 tsp baking powder
>4 oz/100 g vegetable margarine
>2 oz/50 g dried peaches, soaked for an hour in a little water
>1 oz/25 g pumpkin or sunflower seeds
>4 oz/100 g soft brown sugar
>grating of fresh nutmeg
>1 egg
>skimmed milk to mix

Place flours, mixed spice, salt and baking powder in a bowl and rub in the margarine with the tips of your fingers until the mixture resembles fine breadcrumbs. Add the peaches, seeds, sugar and nutmeg. Beat the egg with a little drop of milk, make a well in the centre of the dry ingredients, pour in the egg and milk mixture and gradually combine the liquid with the rest of the ingredients.

Add a little more milk if necessary – the mixture should be fairly stiff in consistency. Place it in a well-greased 6 inch/15 cm cake tin, and bake in a moderate oven (180°C/350°F or gas mark 4) for 50 minutes to one hour.

Pub Lunch

Cold fish with some salad is your best choice of the dishes most likely to be available in a pub at lunch time. Most fish served commercially with salad vegetables is of the oily variety, so sardines, soused herrings (rollmops), smoked mackerel, mackerel pâté, pilchards, tinned salmon and tuna, are likely to be available. Among the cooked variety, fish cakes, hard and soft roe, whitebait and even sprats quite often appear, and are not at all likely to be covered in a layer of batter.

Eat any of these with a wholemeal roll, unbuttered, and select some of the less common green salad vegetables whenever you are lucky enough to find them – curly endive, chicory, raw spinach (ask for this unadorned with bits of fried streaky bacon), and sorrel are all excellent.

Hard-boiled eggs, or an omelette and a bowl of vegetable soup, with low fat cheese, celery and a few radishes also make a good choice. If you are having a white table cloth and silver service lunch and want to appear to drink, choose a non-alcoholic wine, a very low alcohol lager, or a 'Pink Sparkler'. This is made up by placing two or three ice cubes in a glass, adding a few drops of Angostura bitters, and topping up with tonic water and a slice of lemon. Choose a low calorie tonic if you are watching your weight.

Evening Meal

The evening meals suggested here are designed to suit both over-active children and anyone else – child or adult – wanting to include the correct nutrients to enhance both memory and thinking powers. Wherever garlic or herbs are included, simply omit them if cooking for a child who does not like them. But do give them a chance to find out first!

Herrings in oatmeal

Ask the fishmonger to clean and gut the fish – whether the heads remain on is up to you!

one fresh herring, weighing about 7 oz/200 g
salt and pepper
fresh or dried rosemary
safflower oil
1 – 2 oz/25–50 g oatmeal
handful of fresh parsley
¼ lemon

Wipe the herring inside and out, and sprinkle the inside cavity with salt and pepper, and a little rosemary – or place a sprig of the fresh herb inside. Brush the outside of the fish with a very little oil – the books never tell you to do this, 'because herrings are oily', but I can never make the oatmeal stay on otherwise!

Put the oatmeal on a large plate, place the fish in it, and pat the oatmeal on all over its surface using your fingers. Heat the oil until it is very hot (not quite smoking), and place the fish in it, turning once to cook the other side. The flesh cooks easily, and is done when it appears opaque and flakey (about 5 to 7 minutes each side). Remove from pan, drain of excess oil, scoop up all the bits of oatmeal that have fallen off, drain them too, and place on a warm plate. Scatter with the parsley and serve with the lemon.

Some plain boiled potatoes, mashed with a little skimmed milk and some black pepper, and a sliced fresh tomato, are all you need with this rich and tasty dish – apart from some freshly made English mustard!

Calorie count: about 800.

Peachy yoghourt crunch

This is cool and fruity, and naturally sweet – just the right combination of flavours after your oatmealed herring.

1 × 5 oz/150 g carton plain live yoghourt
2 tbsp dried peach purée (see page 90)
2 tbsp homemade muesli (see Moody muesli mark 3, page 90)
ground cinnamon

In a glass dish, place alternate layers of plain yoghourt, peach purée and muesli, starting and ending with the yoghourt. Sprinkle the top with a little cinnamon, and chill very well.

Calorie count: about 125.

Stuffed hearts

Beef hearts are so rich in iron and choline, as well as a wide range of minerals and vitamins that they offer the 'thinking' brain cells excellent nutrition. If you have never tried hearts, it is worth overcoming any suspicion that you may dislike them – many people are pleasantly surprised.

1 beef heart
1 tbsp wholewheat flour, seasoned
1 tbsp safflower oil
10–15 fl oz/300–450 ml vegetable stock

Filling
1 oz/25 g cooked brown rice
1 medium tomato, chopped
1 level tsp dried thyme (or a little more, fresh)
2 tsp pumpkin seeds
1 level tbsp olive or safflower oil
salt and pepper

Rinse the opened heart under the cold water tap, then soak it in cold salted water for an hour. Pat dry on kitchen paper. Mix the filling ingredients together, and stuff into the heart. Tie it up with string, and coat it with the seasoned flour. Heat the oil in a flameproof casserole and brown the heart all over. Add stock, bring to the boil, and cover the casserole. Put it in a moderate oven (180°C/350°F or gas mark 4) and cook for two and a half hours.

Calorie count: about 550.

Some buttered cabbage or spring greens, and some Duchess potatoes (a good source of vitamin C) are nice with this. (For rapid Duchess potatoes, boil and mash some potatoes with a little skimmed milk, place tablespoons of this on a greased baking tray, forking up the tops into peaks for a pretty effect, and place in the oven for the last 45 minutes. You can brown them further under a hot grill for a couple of minutes, if you like).

Baked apple with fruity filling

Use the oven to cook yourself a baked apple to follow this casserole.

>1 large cooking apple
>1 dsp mixed dried fruit
>1 tsp mixed spice
>1 tsp molasses or clear honey

Core the apple, and slit it around its circumference with a sharp knife. Mix the rest of the ingredients, and spoon them into the centre of the fruit. Place in an ovenproof dish, and pour a little water around the apple. Place in oven for one hour while the casserole completes its cooking. Eat with some plain, chilled yoghourt.

Calorie count: about 125.

Spinach and mushroom quiche

You would be unlikely to feel like tackling this quiche from scratch on arriving home from work. However, make it at the weekend and eat some then, saving the rest to eat either warm or cold with a salad or some steamed vegetables. It keeps in the fridge for four to five days.

>8 oz/225 g wholemeal pastry (see page 106)
>2 or 3 tbsp olive or safflower oil
>1 onion, chopped
>1 lb/450g spinach leaves, washed and chopped
>8 oz/225 g mushrooms, roughly chopped
>5 fl oz/150 ml skimmed milk
>3 eggs
>2 oz/50 g cottage cheese
>½ tsp grated nutmeg
>salt and pepper

Line a 9-inch/22.5cm flan tin with the pastry and place on a baking sheet. If you use a metal flan tin, the pastry base will cook through more quickly. Heat the oil and fry the onion; add the washed spinach and mushrooms, stir them around so that they mingle with the hot oil, cover the pan and cook gently for ten minutes. Test them after this time, and cook for a few minutes longer if the mushrooms are not cooked.

Mix the milk, eggs, cheese, nutmeg, and salt and pepper together, add the cooked vegetables, give them a stir, and place in the flan case. Bake in a preheated oven (200°C/400°F or gas mark 6) and bake for 40 to 50 minutes. The quiche is done when the filling is firm and golden coloured. It will provide six servings. This is good with two or three fresh vegetables – lightly buttered, steamed courgettes, new peas or some runner beans go well.

Calorie count: about 385 per serving.

Wholemeal pastry

(8 oz/225 g of pastry means pastry made from 8 oz/25 g of flour plus other ingredients.)

> 8 oz/225 g wholemeal or wholewheat flour
> 2 level tsp baking powder
> pinch salt
> 2 oz/50 g vegetable shortening
> 2 oz/50g vegetable margarine
> 2 tbsp cold water

Mix flour and baking powder and salt in a large bowl. Cut up the fats into small pieces, add them to the flour, and cut them into the dry ingredients with the blade of a knife. Then rub the fat into the flour with your fingertips until it looks like fine breadcrumbs. Add the cold water, mixing it quickly and lightly. Roll the mixture into a ball, put on a sheet of greaseproof paper, put another sheet on top and roll out the pastry to the size you want (this excellent tip came from Rose Elliot, in her book *Simply Delicious*, published by Fontana).

Peel off the top layer of paper, slide your hand under the pastry and the paper layer underneath and lift it, invert the flan case over the bare pastry surface with the other hand, and simply turn the two the reverse way up. This may sound like pure Paul Daniels, but is simply a sure way of getting the pastry into the flan case without fragmenting it!

Charantais melon lake

You can make this dessert with any type of melon that is small enough for one of its halves to be the right size for one person's dessert. Charantais melons have the edge on many of the larger variety, though, for their superb flavour.

> half a ripe Charantais melon
> one small banana, chopped
> a few seedless grapes
> 1 dsp pine kernels
> 1 sherry glass of sweet port or sherry

Remove the seeds from the melon half, and fill its apricot-coloured interior with the fruit, and the pine kernals. These are the seeds of Mediterranean pine trees, and have a mild, sweet, faintly resinous flavour. Pour the liquor over the fruit and eat at once.

Calorie count — about 300.

Here is an idea for a dinner party menu which should please your guests with its unusual ingredients, as well as suiting them should they be either hyperactive or intending to impress you with after-dinner feats of prodigious memory!

Nettle Soup

Nettles (ordinary, common or garden ones) are a delectable vegetable and make wonderful soup. The Romans were so fond of cooked nettles that they brought a variety with them when they conquered Britain so that they would not have to do without a much prized food. They are extremely rich in iron, choline and vitamin C.

Don some thin gloves. Pick young nettle heads in the spring, avoiding any within the reach of passing dogs or too near traffic from which they can absorb noxious fumes. Wash them thoroughly and discard the tough stalks.

> 2 lb/900 g young nettles
> 1 tbsp melted butter
> 1 small onion, chopped
> 2 pints/1.25 l chicken stock
> soured cream
> ½ tsp grated nutmeg

Chicken stock is best for nettle soup, as the flavours blend well. The stock is best made by yourself, by boiling a chicken carcass for a couple of hours together with an onion, carrot and some mixed herbs.

Place butter in a large saucepan, add the chopped onion and fry over a gentle heat for five minutes without letting it brown. Add the nettles, and stir. Cook covered for five to ten minutes, by which time the nettles should have diminished in volume and resemble cooked spinach. Add the chicken stock, bring to the boil, turn down the heat and simmer the soup gently for 20 minutes, watching the liquid level from time to time, and adding a little more stock if necessary. Liquidize, and reheat. Swirl a teaspoon of soured cream in the centre of each bowl, and a little grated nutmeg on top. Serve with warm wholewheat rolls. Serves four.

Calorie count: about 225 per portion with the soured cream.

Homely chicken casserole

Although this casserole is called 'homely', it is perfectly suitable for a dinner party. The flavour of clove permeates the chicken meat, and the broth, which carries the best flavour of all, is so good that most guests request a soup spoon in order to finish every last drop.

> 1 5 lb/2.5 kg chicken
> 2 or 3 strongly-flavoured medium onions
> 9 or 10 cloves
> 6 or 7 medium carrots
> 8 oz/225g any root vegetable (parsnips, swede, turnips)
> 3 or 4 bay leaves
> large pinch each of rosemary, thyme, sage
> salt and white pepper
> 5 fl oz/150 ml white wine

Buy a ready trussed, roasting chicken, preferably fresh. Remove the giblets and wipe it inside and out. Place it in the biggest saucepan you have, and tuck the giblets down the side. Peel the onions (under a running tap), and cut each into quarters. Bruise the heads of the cloves by pressing them down on to a hard surface, then stick them into the onion segments. Lift the chicken and place the onions underneath it.

Prepare and roughly chop the carrots and other root vegetables, and add these with the bay leaves, herbs, salt and pepper to the other ingredients. Pour over the wine, fill the saucepan with boiling water so that most of the ingredients are covered, and cover with a lid. Place over a medium heat, watching until it boils, then turn down the heat so that the liquid remains at a steady though not too vigorous simmer. This takes between two and a half to three hours to cook. Serves four to five hungry people.

The nicest accompaniments are Brussels sprouts, steamed, and mashed with a little vegetable margarine and lots of black pepper, and some plain boiled potatoes.

Calorie count: about 250 per 5 oz/125 g serving.

Gooseberry and avocado delice

The best way to make gooseberry fool is with whipped double cream, rather than with an egg custard — simply because the marriage between the cream and the tart, flavoursome fruit is a perfect one. However, you can substitute crème fraiche, for its far lower fat content, or strained Greek yoghourt if you wish. This recipe includes the mellow richness of avocado, rich in polyunsaturated fats and folic acid.

>1 lb/450 g fresh gooseberries
>3 tbsp light brown sugar
>3 tbsp water
>2 ripe avocado pears
>10 fl oz/300 ml lightly whipped double cream
>3 ripe kiwi fruit, peeled

Put the gooseberries, sugar and water in a pan and simmer for about ten minutes until the fruit is tender. Peel the avocado pears, remove their stones and liquidize them in a blender. Add the stewed fruit to the blender, and blend thoroughly. Remove, place in a bowl and fold in the whipped cream. Spoon into individual glass dishes, and chill thoroughly. Decorate the tops with slices of fresh kiwi fruit.

Calorie count: with cream, about 490 per portion.

Enjoy a Healthy and Active Old Age

Many people think that certain age-related changes in behaviour and mental powers are inevitable. Loss of our intellectual faculties is one of the burdens of old age that many of us most dread, especially if we have come face to face with it in caring for an elderly relative. In fact, though, it is perfectly possible for many people to remain as bright intellectually and as balanced emotionally, into advanced old age, as in their middle years and younger.

This does, of course, mean paying attention to vital factors such as diet, exercise and relaxation during one's prime. For while it is true that brain cells die off at an apparently alarming rate (after the age of twenty, we lose about 50,000 neurones from the cerebral cortex every 24 hours), still the healthy ageing brain manages to compensate to an amazing degree. It is not only geniuses such as Pablo Picasso and Bertrand Russell who retain this ability. The ill effects of arteriosclerosis (hardening of the arteries, resulting in a reduced blood supply), and of malnutrition can be avoided by a balanced diet and lifestyle.

Senility, with its absent-mindedness, depression, tendency to repeat statements, irrational behaviour, poor muscular coordination and defective memory, is related directly to arteriosclerosis, poor diet and factors such as prolonged stress, the misuse of alcohol and drugs, and toxic metals, in particular aluminium. The condition affects around five per cent of people above the age of sixty-five and at least ten per cent of those over seventy-five. These estimates are likely to be conservative, as they do not include the many undiagnosed cases of mild senility.

In a study of 260 'healthy' people between the ages of sixty and ninety-four, all of higher than average educational standard, the ten to fifteen per cent with the worst diets from the nutritional points of view were also those showing greatest memory impairment and intellectual powers. Loss of brain cells from the hypothalamus, which controls the body's hormonal system, affects nearly all our bodily functions, and loss from this area is bound to be reflected in declining well-being in other systems. A high protein diet speeds up this decline, and this is a further reason for keeping protein intake to a healthy minimum.

In some cases, however, *deficiency* of protein is one of the culprits. Many older people think of red meat as the only 'real' source of protein, and it is this dietary item that can prove most costly to elderly people on a low budget. Meat also requires careful cooking, and the expenditure of time, effort and money on fuel and preparation. For many elderly people living alone, a white bread sandwich, with jam or marmalade, or a packet of sweet biscuits, (with numerous cups of sweet tea) is the type of diet they eventually come to rely upon. This intake is dangerously low in essential protein, so it is not surprising that the manufacture of vital brain neurotransmitters is adversely affected.

More and more gerontologists (experts in human ageing) are now coming to pay serious attention to the injurious effects of two biochemical processes, free radical formation and lipid peroxidation, which are now thought to be a major cause of senile changes because of their profound effects on the degeneration of cells in the body and brain.

When food fuel is metabolized, energy is released from it by chemical action involving the transfer of negatively charged particles, electrons. This is happening throughout all the tissues of the body, all the time we are alive. But highly reactive, potentially noxious atoms of molecules called 'free radicals' are also generated by the process of energy-release. While the formation of these free radicals is necessary to life, things can get seriously out of hand when too many are formed. They can destabilize ordinary, balanced molecules, turning them into further free radicals. This can take place on a large scale in a series of chain reactions, with more anddmore unstable particles being generated.

Free radical activity can result in damage to the immune system. It can also adversely affect the genetic material, DNA, in cells, distorting the information required for normal reduplication. A major aspect of the ageing process is the gradual failure of cells to reproduce themselves as perfect replicas before their lifespan comes to an end. One of the causes of this degenerative process is free radical activity.

Part of the ageing process of the brain consists of an increasing inability to reform dendrites, the filaments at the ends of adjacent neurones. The unopposed destructive activity of free radical formation is in part responsible. Free radicals also attack the lipids that form a vital part of every cell membrane throughout the body, but they have a particular chance to wreak havoc in the brain because of its high lipid (fat) content. When this change occurs, damage is caused to brain tissue that has been directly related by a number of scientists to the development of senile dementia.

I should add at this point that many doctors now believe that there is a connection between the development of senile dementia (in particular with the form of presenile dementia known as Alzheimer's disease) and aluminium toxicity. It is therefore safer not to use aluminium cooking utensils, and to avoid other known sources of it such as foil wrapping for food, antacids for indigestion, baking powder and deodorants. Aluminium is also used as an emulsifier for certain processed cheeses, and is often found in table salt and white flour, as it has a bleaching effect.

Which Foods?

A balanced wholefood diet may in practice terms be an impossibility for many old people, unless specifically tailored to their needs. Apart from cost, many elderly people have poor digestions, false teeth (which makes chewing seeds, nuts and raw vegetables extremely difficult) and, even more of a problem, no wish to alter the way they have always bought and prepared food. However, here are some suggestions for overcoming these problems. A change from 'wrapped, sliced, white cotton wool' to wholemeal bread should not be too difficult. Kidney, heart and calves' or lambs' liver are cheaper than red meat, offer good food value, and take far less time to cook. Eggs and low-fat cheese are also 'easy' protein sources, as are individual portions of white or oily fish (many of which can be bought 'boil in the bag'), and chicken quarters.

Chopped or grated salad vegetables are often acceptable, and finely-milled nuts and seeds can be stored for two weeks in a closed container in the fridge or larder, to be used as a salad or soup sprinkle.

Soups made from fresh vegetables and the freshly squeezed juice of fruit and vegetables are another ideal way of elderly and infirm people getting their daily minerals and vitamins in an attractive form. Liquidizing steamed or boiled vegetables, and adding a little yeast extract and low sodium salt, herbs and skimmed milk, is well within the scope of many old people living alone. It sometimes happens that, once they have become interested in food preparation again, they feel the benefit of dietary change soon enough to become thoroughly enthusiastic about it.

Grains, pulses and dried beans – such rich sources of nutrients and fibre – need not represent a stumbling block, either. These, after all, have been used since time immemorial, and most of us are used to adding pearl barley, rice, lentils or butter beans to a stew or casserole. When catering for a sick old person, or organizing someone else to do so, the role of the liquidizer in 'solid' food preparation as well as that of soups, should be remembered.

Boiled lentils (which do not require presoaking), can be made into a delicious and highly nutritious purée that is perfectly easy both to swallow without chewing and to digest. This is only a short step from substituting split peas, haricot beans, continental lentils and other pulses on future occasions. Plenty of ideas are provided in the recipes.

Dr Abram Hoffer, a Canadian gerontologist who has been treating senile patients with dietary improvements and supplementary vitamins and minerals for over thirty years, is convinced that the specific anti-ageing and anti-senility nutrients are those that protect the tissues from excessive oxidation. In addition to a well balanced diet, the nutrients to which he attaches special importance include the B complex vitamins (especially B 1 and B 3), vitamins A, C and E, zinc and selenium.

Also known for their ability to combat the ill effects of abnormal oxidation, are the amino acid compound glutathione (made from three amino acids, glycine, cysteine and glutamic acid), and the sulphur-containing amino acid methionine (from which the other sulphur-rich amino acids taurine, cysteine and cystine are made). Extra potassium should also be remembered, as well as a source of sulphur to aid amino acid synthesis. And the need of elderly people for choline, lecithin and inositol is paramount.

Food sources for vitamins B, A, C and E are shown in the table on page 197. **Selenium** is found in wheat germ, tomatoes, onions, broccoli and tuna fish. **Sulphur** is provided by egg yolk, beef, fish, eggs and cabbage, as well as dried beans. **Potassium** is found in all green leafy vegetables, tomatoes, mint, potatoes, watercress and bananas. Many elderly people are potassium deficient, due to the effect of high blood pressure drugs (diuretics), watery stools (due to misuse of laxatives or chronic diarrhoea), and to poor diet. Effects are muscular weakness, depression, mild confusion, and when very severe, the heart is affected.

Good sources of **methionine** include cod, cottage cheese, shrimps, trout, liver and lamb. Two others are pumpkin seeds and sesame seeds. **Cystine** is found in dried, low fat milk, eggs, turkey, peanut butter and oatmeal.

The enzyme **SOD** (superoxide dismutase) occurs in all our body cells. It affords protection to DNA and the immune system, in this way helping to guard against the effects of radiation, the development of cancer, and the degenerative processes of old age. SOD is available as a nutritional supplement, but the best dietary approach is to include as much raw food in the diet as possible, since that is a rich source of the enzyme. Freshly squeezed vegetable and fruit juices are also an excellent source of SOD.

Finally, there is some evidence that deteriorating (ageing) cells can be partly rejuvenated if provided with the nucleic acids DNA and RNA which nourish them in a special way. By helping the body to stay well supplied with nucleic acids. Dr Benjamin S Frank, author of *Nucleic Acid Therapy in Ageing and Disease* (Psychological Library, 1969, revised 1974) has found that you can look and feel six to twelve years younger than you actually are. Foods that are rich in nucleic acids include wheat, germ, bran, spinach, asparagus, mushrooms, fish (especially sardines, salmon and anchovies), chicken liver, oatmeal and onions.

Dr Franks recommends a diet in which sea food is eaten seven times a week, along with two glasses of skimmed milk, a glass of fruit or vegetable juice and four glasses of water daily, he also recommends RNA/DNA supplementation, available from health food shops and suppliers.

Recipes

The recipes in this section are designed in the main for elderly people who either are able to prepare their own food, or have a friend or relation to prepare food for them, but I am also including hints for those who live alone and depend upon a 'meals on wheels' service. These meals rarely contain wholefoods, however carefully prepared, but there is every reason why those who use the service should eat all the good things these meals provide, and supplement them with easy-to-eat products which they can include in their shopping lists. For this reason, in this chapter only, I have suggested buying a number of ready-prepared foods, tinned, frozen and packaged.

Just a few basic items provide a wide range of the nutrients needed by elderly people. If you eat a thin slice of wholemeal bread, margarine or butter, and smooth peanut butter or cottage cheese, instead of white bread, margarine and jam you substantially increase your intake of numerous vital nutrients. These include choline, the nucleic acids, pantothenic acid, selenium, zinc, niacin, vitamin E, cystine, vitamin A, vitamin B6, inositol, folic acid and calcium, to name only some of them!

However, many of us, particularly when we grow older, stick like barnacles to long-established eating patterns, and it is unrealistic to expect complete alterations in diet. So any projected food changes have to be made gradually and subtly.

Breakfast

The 'early morning cuppa' is a vital start to the day for many. This is best made as weak as is acceptable to the taste buds, using skimmed milk and a little clear honey if necessary. A number of healthy tisanes available from health food shops may appeal to you as an 'ordinary' tea drinker, especially those based on fruit and dried flowers. Teas made from rosehips, oranges, apples, passion flowers and a wide variety of herbs offer a very pleasing alternative to Indian teas.

Maurice Meségué, in his book *Health Secrets of Plants and Herbs* (Pan), suggests the following simple preparation which is both good to drink and offers some protection against arteriosclerosis (hardening of the arteries). One pinch each of marjoram, sage and mint (all common, household herbs) are infused in a cup of boiling water, as described in the directions for lemon balm tea on page 31.

Fresh juices

If you do not already have an electric centrifuge juicer as described earlier in this book, I do recommend your buying one if you can. The initial outlay will be repaid many times over in terms of the enormous health benefits of freshly prepared juice drinks.

Carrot and celery juice

This juice combination not only provides many vitamins and minerals, it is also a recognized form of juice therapy for arthritis as recommended by John B. Lust in his book *Raw Juice Therapy* (Thorsons Publishers, 1959).

Juice enough scrubbed carrots and washed celery to produce 8 fl oz/250 ml of each juice, mix them, and serve, with ice cubes if you like.

Calorie count: about 90.

Carrot, beetroot and cucumber

This combination is equally pleasant first thing, and is recommended to help correct anaemia. Juice sufficient of these vegetables to produce 6 fl oz/175 ml of carrot juice, and 5 fl oz/150 ml each of beetroot and cucumber. Chill, stir and serve.

Calorie count: about 130.

If you have no juicer, try a 5 fl oz/150 ml glass of unsweetened canned or carton grapefruit, tomato, apple, pineapple or orange juice first thing. If the grapefruit juice seems too sharp, mix it half and half with either orange or apple. You can pep up tomato juice with a few drops of Worcestershire sauce or a little black pepper.

Morning melon

Melons are naturally very sweet when ripe, and require little chewing! Buy one when they are cheap, and eat as follows:

> 6 oz/175 g slice melon
> 1 small banana, or half a large one
> 1 dsp wheatgerm

Remove melon seeds, cut the flesh into medium sized chunks, chop the banana and mix the two together, adding the wheatgerm, and serve. Alternatively, liquidize the ingredients with 10 fl oz/300 ml skimmed milk, pour into a tall glass with ice cubes and serve.

Calorie count: about 120 without the milk, 220 with milk.

I can also recommend the 'Egg energizer' drink (page 33) and the 'Soya milk breakfast' (page 34). Eat a piece of fresh fruit with either of these. If nuts and seeds do not appeal to you, try a little fruit purée as suggested under 'Soya milk breakfast', using either apricots or peaches (method as for 'Apricot Astarte', page 35). You can use either the dried or the fresh fruit, or any soft fruit in season. Try a glass of nut milk if you are feeling adventurous (see page 34). If you would prefer it sweeter, omit the lemon juice and stir in a dessertspoon of clear honey or molasses.

Just to show you that nut milk drinks are not a new-fangled 'health crank' idea, here is a very similar recipe to those I have given. It appeared in the 'Cooking for invalids' section of the Daily Express book *Economical Cookery*. My edition is falling apart with age and no publication date is apparent, but a time earlier this century is indicated by the prices of the foods, e.g. half a packet of cereal, threepence halfpenny, grapefruit fourpence each, and a pigeon, tenpence!

Almond restorative

> 3 oz/75 g almonds
> 1 tbsp cream
> 1 pint/600 ml milk
> sugar to taste

Blanch, skin and shred the almonds. Then pound with the cream until smooth. Add milk and sweetening. Allow to stand for half an hour, strain and serve.

Moody muesli, mark 4

If you do enjoy something chewy and filling at breakfast time, try the following muesli. This one contains more wheat germ than the others I have given recipes for, as it is so rich in selenium, zinc, vitamins B 3 and E, and nucleic acids.

> 1 tbsp porridge oats
> 2 tbsp wheat germ
> 1 tbsp raisins
> chopped segments of 1 orange
> half a banana, mashed
> sprinkling of pumpkin seeds (optional)
> skimmed milk or fresh orange juice (optional)

Place the oats, wheat germ and raisins in a small dish, chop up the orange flesh letting all the juice fall into the dish, and add to the cereal. Mix and leave overnight. In the morning, mash half a banana (you can use the second half in a sandwich, later), mix it into the muesli, and add the seeds if you are using them. Add a little skimmed milk or fresh orange juice if you like.

Calorie count: about 410 without the seeds, 520 with them.

Eggs are one of the cheapest sources of protein and one of the easiest to cook. A lightly boiled egg with soldiers of wholewheat bread or toast, lightly spread with butter or margarine, provides some vital vitamin B 12 and B 6, inositol, SOD and a range of other nutrients. Coddled eggs are said to be more easily digested than soft boiled ones, and are even easier to prepare, if possible.

Coddled eggs

To coddle an egg, place a (preferably new laid) egg in its shell, in a cup or small basin and pour boiling water over it. Leave it to stand in a warm place for about six minutes. It is then ready to eat.

Calorie count: about 80.

A piece of smoked haddock makes a pleasant change. If you buy your fish from a fishmonger, ask either for a piece of genuine Finnan haddock, which has the best flavour of all, or a 'golden slice', which is the name often given to small smoked haddock fillets, just the right size for one person. Poach your haddock in a little water for about ten minutes and eat with a little margarine and a warm milk bap (see below).

If you do not have a fishmonger in your area, use a packet of frozen smoked haddock. These are usually enough for two, and since they are 'boil in the bag', cook both together and save the other for another meal or a lunchtime sandwich filling (see below).

Milk baps

If you enjoy baking, try this recipe. The soya flour helps to lighten the dough and supplies extra protein.

1½ tbsp light brown sugar
½ oz/15 g yeast

11 fl oz/325 ml tepid whole milk
12 oz/350 g wholewheat flour
4 oz/100 g soya flour
1 tsp salt
2 oz/50 g melted margarine

Mix 1 teaspoon of sugar with the yeast and 2 tablespoons of the milk to form a paste, and stand in a warm place until it is frothy. Mix flours, salt and remaining sugar in a large warm bowl, add the yeast liquid, the rest of the milk, and the melted margarine, and mix the dough until it is smooth. Knead it on a floured tabletop until it is smooth and elastic, and set aside in a warm place for an hour until the dough has doubled its size.

Remove from bowl, knead it again for 5 minutes, divide it into twelve rolls and set on a lightly oiled baking tray. Leave again in a warm place until the volume of the rolls has again increased to nearly twice the size.

Place the tray in an oven preheated to very hot (230° C/ 450° F or gas mark 8) and reduce the temperature after 15 minutes to 220° C/425° F or gas mark 7, for a further five to ten minutes. Remove from the oven, and cool on a wire rack.

Calorie count: about 245 per roll.

Lunch

If you have retired, then instead of having to cope with packed 'working' lunches, you are more likely to need ideas for light meals at home – again, these are all interchangeable with the evening meal. Being at home does mean that you have the choice of cooking if you feel like it, so I have included one or two ideas taking this into account.

Salads are still vital for you, though, since raw vegetables, fruit, nuts and seeds offer such a vast range of vital ingredients to help keep you young and active. So I have suggested several salad meals based on grains and pulses comparable to those appearing in the other sections.

Sweetcorn, bean and tuna salad

This salad combines a grain you are bound to be familiar with – sweetcorn – with red kidney beans which provide calcium and tuna fish which gives you selenium and the vital brain nutrient DHA.

>2 oz/50 g red kidney beans (canned, or dried, soaked and cooked)
>2 oz/50 g canned or frozen sweetcorn
>short length of cucumber
>1 medium tomato
>small can of tuna fish
>half a punnet of mustard and cress
>yoghourt and chervil dressing (see below)

Drain the beans and sweetcorn, mix in a bowl, slice the cucumber and tomato, and mix into the vegetable together with the drained, flaked tuna fish. Sprinkle the cress on top. Toss in the dressing.

Add a hard-boiled egg if you are very hungry, for extra protein, and eat with a lightly buttered milk bap (see page 120).

Calorie count: about 360 without the egg, 440 with egg.

Yoghourt and chervil dressing

>2 tbsp plain yoghourt
>2 tsp clear honey
>2 tsp cider vinegar
>salt and pepper
>1 dsp fresh chervil leaves or half tsp dried

Mix the yoghourt, honey and cider vinegar together, season lightly and mix in the chervil. If you have no chervil, use either sweet basil or marjoram.

Macaroni coleslaw salad

Either buy the quickly cooked, short length macaroni or, better still, try the wholewheat variety and chop it up when it is cooked.

>2 oz/50 g dry macaroni
>the heart of a young cabbage
>half a small onion
>2 medium carrots
>1 tbsp raisins or sultanas
>1 tbsp unsalted peanuts (optional)
>cider vinegar dressing (page 40)

Cook the macaroni until it is soft but not flabby. If you use the wholewheat type, rinse well under a warm tap. Drain, and place in a bowl. Finely shred as much cabbage heart as you think you will need, grate the onion (this makes the coleslaw much moister), and grate the carrots. Mix these into the pasta, together with the raisins and nuts, if using. Pour over the cider vinegar dressing, and mix well in. This is nice with a slice or two of crispbread, lightly spread with butter or margarine, and some cold, cooked smoked haddock (see page 120).

Calorie count: about 310 without the nuts, 460 with them.

Green vitality salad

This salad is really easy, and very high in the vitamins and minerals you most need.

>small bunch watercress
>mustard and cress
>2 or 3 'inside' lettuce leaves
>3 or 4 finely chopped spring onions
>2 or 3 cold potatoes, diced
>1 or 2 tbsp salad cream

Finely shred the watercress, mustard and cress and lettuce leaves, and mix them with the chopped spring onions and the diced cold potatoes (the waxy type are better for this than the floury variety). Mix in the salad cream, and eat with a milk bap and a slice of cold beef, or some cold chicken.

Calorie count: about 150.

Sandwiches

Try the following sandwich fillings. You can eat them between slices of wholewheat bread, inside rolls, on slices of rye bread, crispbread or crackers as open sandwiches, or in warmed pitta bread.

1 mashed banana with some low fat cheese, a teaspoon of clear honey and a little ground cinnamon.

2 an ounce or two of grated Cheddar cheese, with a teaspoon of beef extract and a sliced tomato.

3 some grated apple, with a grating of nutmeg, some very finely chopped Brazil nuts or hazel nuts, and a dessertspoon of cottage cheese, well drained.

4 finely minced roast beef or veal or cold pork, with a little grated onion and thinly sliced cucumber.

5 tahini, well stirred to distribute its oil content, with a teaspoon of molasses, and a teaspoon of wheat germ.

6 a hard-boiled egg, mashed with one or two drained sardines and some thinly sliced tomato.

If you feel like something warm and tasty, don't forget that most sandwiches toast well. Eaten with soup, a glass of fruit juice or milk, and a piece of fruit or some fruit purée, they make a filling light meal. Here is my own recipe for an even tastier than usual Welsh rarebit, which can be most welcome on a cold day.

Boozy Welsh rarebit

1 oz/25 g margarine
half tsp mustard
salt, pepper, nutmeg
2 tbsp barley wine
3 oz/75 g really strong Cheddar cheese, grated
1 or 2 slices wholemeal toast, lightly buttered

Mix the margarine, mustard, seasoning, nutmeg, wine and cheese together and heat gently in a small saucepan, stirring, until the cheese has melted and amalgamated with the rest. When it starts to bubble, spoon immediately on to your toast and eat. This Welsh rarebit will be a bit more liquid than the usual variety, but the taste more than makes up for it.

Finally, two soup recipes that are quick and inexpensive to make.

Onion and potato soup

Together with an electric juicer, a blender has to be the best culinary friend of anyone wanting to feed well on a limited budget yet with little inclination to spend backbreaking hours in the kitchen. Soups made from fresh ingredients are not only nutritious and sustaining, they are also easy to eat and can tempt the appetite when solid food has lost its appeal.

2 or 3 medium sized potatoes
a large onion
vegetable, chicken or meat stock or water
salt and pepper
milk or evaporated milk to taste
Worcestershire sauce

Peel and chop the potatoes up, peel and slice the onion

finely, and place all the vegetables in a large saucepan with enough water or stock to cover well. Bring to boiling point, turn down the heat and simmer until the vegetables are cooked (about 20 to 25 minutes). Put in blender, liquidize, and return to the saucepan. Add a little milk or evaporated milk to bring it to the consistency you require, season with the pepper and salt, and serve, with a few drops of Worcestershire sauce.

Calorie count: about 250, including the milk.

Brussels sprout soup

This is made in almost exactly the same way, except that with a well-flavoured stock there is no need to include onion unless you wish to. The most economical way to cook this and many other vegetable soups is to cook more vegetables than you require for a hot meal, and heat up the left-over veg the next day with some stock.

> 8 oz/225 g cold cooked Brussels sprouts
> 10 – 15 fl oz/300–450 ml well flavoured stock
> some fresh or evaporated milk
> salt and pepper
> grating of nutmeg (essential, unless you dislike it!)

Bring the sprouts to the boil in the stock, turn down the heat and simmer for a few minutes until the vegetables are heated through. Liquidize in blender, return to saucepan, add as much milk as you require, and then season with the salt, pepper and nutmeg.

Calorie count: about 250 to 300 including the milk.

Most dried pulses make very pleasant soups. You might especially like to try the lentil soup for which I have already given a recipe (see page 43). Broccoli soup is also chock-full of the nutrients you specially require (see page 100).

Evening Meal

Have you ever tried sweetbreads? When you can get them, buy them and give them a go! In fact they are delicious, and far from being some mysterious and unmentionable organ of the lamb or calf, they are in fact the animal's pancreas or occasionally its thymus gland – full to the brim of protein and no different from eating the heart, kidney or liver. They are also very digestible.

Sautéed sweetbreads

3 – 4 oz/75–100 g sweetbreads
1 beaten egg
salt and pepper
half tsp dried sage
2 or 3 tbsp wholemeal breadcrumbs
safflower oil for cooking
1 tbsp chopped parsley

Drop the sweetbreads in boiling water for 1 minute to blanch them, then remove, cool, and trim away any fat or gristly bits. Mix the beaten egg with the salt, pepper and sage, dip the sweetbreads in it, coat with the breadcrumbs and press them on well to form a coat. Heat the oil in a frying pan and, when very hot, fry the sweetbreads on both sides until they are golden brown. Drain them on kitchen paper to remove as much oil as possible, and serve, garnished with the parsley. Sweetbreads are nice with mashed potato and peas.

Calorie count: about 640.

Here is a delicious, light pudding to follow the sweetbreads. Make a sponge in your usual way, or buy a plain sponge cake and cut it into slices.

Sponge fruit pudding

2 cooking apples
1 tbsp honey
10 very thin slices of plain sponge cake
1 egg
5 fl oz/150 ml skimmed or whole milk

Peel and core the apples, and stew them with a little water and the honey until they are soft and mushy. Line a 1 pint/600 ml pie dish with half the sponge slices, cover with the pulped apple, then cover this with the remaining sponge slices. Beat the egg, add the milk, and pour over the pudding. Bake in the oven preheated to 180°C/350°F or gas mark 4 for 15 to 20 minutes. Serve with a little evaporated milk.

Calorie count: about 540 without the evaporated milk, 600 with the milk.

Steamed whiting

Whiting has two things in common with sweetbreads – it is very nutritious, and much underrated! Some influential person in the public eye must once have referred to whiting as cat food. In fact, it is quite delicious, and now is the time to appreciate it, for once top chefs have become reacquainted with its delicate flavour, its price will soar!

1 small filleted whiting
pepper and salt
juice of ½ lemon
½ tsp dill weed

Sprinkle the surface of the whiting with salt, pepper, lemon juice and the dill weed. Place it on a large plate, dot its surface with small pieces of margarine, and cover with a saucepan lid. Place this over a saucepan of boiling water, and leave until the fish is opaque (about 12 to 15 minutes).

This is nice with some new buttered carrots, a few peas, and some plain boiled potatoes.

Calorie count: about 350.

Banana custard

Make up a custard in the usual way. Slice a banana, place in the bottom of a dish and pour the custard over it. Eat when cool with a little evaporated milk or single cream

Calorie count: about 450.

Here is a very simple vegetarian dish you are doubtless familiar with. Choose a fresh-looking cauliflower, small enough to suit your requirements.

Cauliflower cheese

1 small cauliflower
2 oz/50 g margarine
2 tbsp wholemeal flour
15 fl oz/450 ml milk
4 oz/100 g grated strong Cheddar cheese
pepper, salt, a little mustard

Divide the cauliflower into three or four parts, and either steam or boil until tender but not mushy in a little fast-boiling water. Melt the margarine, stir in the flour, cook slowly for two or three minutes, stir in the milk carefully, stirring all the time to avoid lumps, then cook gently for 7 to 10 minutes. Add most of the cheese, and the pepper, salt and mustard. Drain the cauliflower when it is cooked, place in a heatproof dish, pour the sauce over it, and sprinkle on the rest of the cheese. Brown under the grill and serve at once. Enough for 2 helpings.

Calorie count: about 650 per serving.

Here is a good meal to serve when you feel like entertaining. It does not take hours to prepare, it is not expensive, and – even more to the point – it is tasty enough for your guests to be sure to ask you for recipes.

Asparagus

1 large onion
1 tbsp safflower oil
3 or 4 medium potatoes, chopped
1 small tin asparagus
1½ pints/900 ml chicken stock
salt and pepper
evaporated milk to mix
juice of ½ fresh lemon

Chop the onion, fry it gently in the oil for ten minutes, then add the potatoes, roughly chopped. Cook for 1 minute, then pour in the stock, season with pepper and salt, bring to the boil, then simmer gently for 25 minutes. Add the asparagus spears with the juice from their tin, about 10 minutes before the potatoes are done. Liquidize in the blender, return to the saucepan, add some evaporated milk, tasting as you go, and reheat. Add a squeeze of lemon juice, and serve, with dry, thinly sliced wholemeal toast. Serves four.

Calorie count: about 150 per serving.

Game creams

These sound as though they ought to be served at the Ritz. In fact, they are cheap, although delectable, and easy to make.

2 sachets gelatine
10 fl oz/300 ml boiling water
10 fl oz/300 ml chicken stock
5 oz/150 g minced rabbit

salt and pepper
1 tbsp evaporated milk
4 thin slices tomato

Sprinkle the gelatine onto the boiling water in a small bowl. Set the bowl over a pan of boiling water and stir gently until the gelatine has dissolved. Bring the chicken stock to the boil, cool slightly, then stir in the gelatine, and add the rabbit, seasoning, and evaporated milk. Place a slice of tomato in the base of each of four wetted moulds, pour in the mixture and allow to set. When ready to serve, dip the bottoms of the moulds into warm water, and turn out. Serves four. Game creams are nice served with cold potato salad, dressed with a lemony mayonnaise, and some cold, sliced beetroot with cider vinegar dressing.

Calorie count: about 200 per serving.

Bread and butter pudding

This may be an old nursery favourite, but it is gaining popularity again in many well-known London restaurants. Make it with single cream as a very special treat for favourite guests – otherwise, use skimmed milk and cut down on saturated fats! A little stewed fruit goes nicely with this.

4 thin slices wholewheat bread, buttered
1 oz/25 g sultanas or raisins
1 oz/25 g currants
1½ oz/40 g brown sugar
small pinch of salt
1 egg
10 fl oz/300 ml milk or single cream
grinding of nutmeg

Line a greased pie dish with half the bread and butter slices, add the fruit and brown sugar, cover with the rest of the bread. Beat up the egg with the milk and salt, and pour over the contents of the dish. Grate the nutmeg over it, leave it to soak for half an hour, then bake it in a moderate oven (180°C/350°F or gas mark 4). Serves four.

Calorie count: about 300 with milk, 470 with single cream.

Improve Your Physical Stamina and Pain Resistance

Stamina

Physical stamina may seem an odd thing to write about in a book about mood and food. However, physical well-being and the emotions are so inextricably interrelated, and physical fatigue has so profound an effect upon mood and behaviour, that there is every reason to offer some advice on coping with bodily stress.

Not, of course, that it is ever possible to consider physical stress as an isolated entity. Any factor or group of factors can overtax the body, deplete our overall resources, cause fatigue, and engender a degree of emotional strain at the same time. Frequently, in fact, the physical and emotional stress components of a situation exert equal influence.

Take, for example, a number of familiar, physically tiring occupations. Working full time, and returning to care for house, husband and family, can be physically extremely wearing. Looking after babies and/or energetic toddlers all day – particularly in confined quarters – can tax your physical resources and emotional calm to their furthest limit. Similarly, working long office or factory hours while trying to learn the job and act efficiently can bring you metaphorically to your knees by the time you are ready to commute home through the rush hour.

Which Foods?

We have already looked at stress, anxiety and insomnia, all of which may play parts in a physically demanding life style, and have seen the best foods to eat in order to combat their effects. In the present section, we are going to see which nutrients are best able to protect us from stress that is primarily physical, by increasing energy levels.

Amino acids are a vital aspect of an overall balanced diet for 'high demand' activity. Athletes and sportsmen and women are scrupulously careful to see that they take in enough protein daily to provide for their requirements — all of which are noticeably increased by hard physical labour, sports practice and aerobic exercise. The body's metabolic processes turn to its own tissues, and break them down to supply energy when given insufficient fuel. Eating 'as normal', yet greatly increasing one's energy output by demanding exercise, has the same effect. Supply *must* meet demand, and it is vital to give the body enough fuel to suit its requirements. This is the only way to remain healthy and balanced.

Vitamins A, B complex, C and E are all highly important to high exercise regimens. Vitamin C, is essential to the formation of strong, resilient collagen, one the body's vital connective tissues which is subjected to proportionately more strain whenever the body works extra hard physicallly. It is also vital for the repair of body tissues, strong blood vessels and bones and it helps guard againt the depleting effects of all forms of extra stress.

The B vitamins help us to obtain energy from our food by aiding the breakdown of carbohydrates into glucose, and by helping in the production of healthy red cells in the blood, responsible for the transport of oxygen from the lungs to the tissues. It is especially important, if you are exercising heavily or doing very tiring work, to avoid the tempting energy boost refined carbohydrate snacks can provide. The last thing you need is reactive hypoglycaemia in response to initial overloading of the blood with the glucose, leaving you weak, trembly and shaking just when you most need to give of your best.

Vitamin E is vital to those engaged in heavy exercise. It protects the good health of the heart and cardiovascular system generally, helping to see that tissues receive their oxygen when needed. It also acts in its antioxidant capacity at a time when most required, since aerobic exercises increases the need for antioxidant activity. Moreover, vitamin E exerts an anticramp-like action on muscles, vital when you are exercising.

The foods that supply these vitamins are shown in the table on pages 196–200.

Iron and **zinc** are essential minerals. Zinc governs the contractility of muscle and deficiency can cause fatigue and lethargy. Iron is essential to help guard against fatigue when physical conditions are very demanding. As we saw with intelligence and learning ability, it is not necessary to have a demonstrable iron deficiency anaemia, to need more of this element than you are getting. Physically taxing work increases the need for iron subtly and inexorably.

Octacosanol is an energy sustainer, and tests have shown that it has dramatic effects upon athletic stamina. It may also have a protective effect against heart strain and speed up reaction time. It is a natural food substance present in vegetable oil, wheat, wheat germ and its oil, and alfalfa leaves. It has a nauseating taste when taken as a supplement – the usual instruction is to chew the tablets. Increasing your intake of the foods rich in this nutrient, and eating them regularly, should have a more permanent effect.

Pain

Chronic pain seriously affects how a person feels and behaves. This may seem an obvious statement, but prolonged periods of pain are fortunately not everyone's experience. It can be only too easy to think that painkilling drugs have become so sophisticated, that people don't actually experience much pain at all. This is far from the case; chronic pain patients represent major diagnostic and treatment dilemmas for health professionals of all kinds.

Since the neurotransmitter serotonin is known to be associated with the pain experience (the higher the serotonin brain levels, the greater the pain threshold), many trials have been carried out into the potential of serotonin's precursor tryptophan as a natural method of pain relief.

Tryptophan-enriched diets have been found to reduce depression and increase pain tolerance in chronic pain patients, and to increase the pain relief gained from electrical stimulatory methods. Conversely, tryptophan-poor diets have been found to decrease brain serotonin, and to decrease pain thresholds.

Some research workers feel that the best way of relieving pain with tryptophan may be to combine daily doses of pure tryptophan with a low protein, low fat, high carbohydrate diet. This approach has been shown to produce 'significantly raised pain tolerance thresholds in normal subjects'.

Recipes

The following recipes and meal ideas are designed to boost physical stamina in general, and to be of special help when extra demands are being made on you. The specially high level of physical stamina you require if you are in sports training, would certainly be boosted by the types of food I suggest, but I would recommend your sports trainer as the best qualified person to give advice in this respect. He or she knows you as an individual, and is aware both of your own personal level of physical fitness and of the particular demands being made on you at any one time.

In these recipes, then, there will be an emphasis upon obtaining the essential amino acids, either from first class protein, or from a combination of vegetable foods. I am also setting out to include foods with the following stamina-providing nutrients – vitamins A, C, E and B complex, the minerals iron, zinc, potassium and magnesium, and octacosanol.

Breakfast

Sage and marjoram tea has a reputation for being a good pep-up tonic. A large number of herbs have, of course, including ginseng which I regard more as a form of herbal medicine, to be taken as a course for two or three weeks. Sage and marjoram are herbs you are likely to have in the kitchen, so brew a cup of herbal tea from them to drink first thing, instead of tea or coffee.

1½ tsp dried sage
½ tsp dried marjoram
large slice of lemon
a little honey to taste

Method – see instructions for lemon balm tea, page 31.

Fresh Juices

Dr John B. Lust recommends the fresh juices of carrots, celery, apple, beetroot and cucumber as energy givers, in his book *Raw Juice Therapy*. He suggests that they be taken in the following amounts and combinations:

carrot and celery juice, 8 fl oz/250 ml of each
carrot and apple juice 8 fl oz/250 ml
carrot juice 6 fl oz/200 ml with 5 fl oz/150 ml each of beetroot and cucumber

Bridget Amies, in her book *Fruit and Vegetable Juices* (Academy Publications Ltd.) suggests a number of juice recipes that act as 'general vitalizers'. She says that any of them can be taken as a substitute for a meal, providing that a glass of nut milk is taken as well. If you do require a great deal of physical stamina and yet have never been able to face breakfast, I endorse her suggestion heartily. Here are three of her favourites:

1. 6 tbsp beetroot juice
   1 tbsp onion juice
   1 tsp finely chopped parsley (to sprinkle on the top)
   sprinkling of paprika pepper

2. 6 tbsp tomato juice
   2 tsp lemon juice
   1 tbsp cream
   1 tsp finely chopped parsley

3. 6 tbsp radish juice
   1 tbsp cream
   1 tsp finely chopped mint.

Hot citrus surprise

The 'surprise' consists in having hot grapefruit for breakfast. Most people think of it as a quickly prepared starter to a dinner party, served with brown sugar and sherry. But citrus fruit provides vitamin C, magnesium and potassium, all vital stamina nutrients, so makes an excellent start to the day. (The pumpkin seeds provide zinc, too.)

> ½ large grapefruit
> 1 small tangerine or satsuma
> 1 tbsp pumpkin seeds
> 2 tbsp plain yoghourt
> 1 dsp clear honey or molasses
> juice of ½ lemon
> 2 tsp wheat germ

Scrape the flesh from the grapefruit half, peel and segment the tangerine or satsuma and add to the grapefruit flesh, mix in the seeds, yoghourt, honey or molasses, and lemon juice. Heat gently in a small saucepan until very hot, pile back in the grapefruit skin, scatter with the wheat germ and serve.

Calorie count: about 250.

Fig and almond milk shake

This uses two nut varieties, almonds and peanuts, rich in protein and magnesium. Figs also supply magnesium.

> 2 or 3 dried figs, soaked overnight
> 15 fl oz/450 ml almond nut milk
> 1 tbsp molasses
> 1 tbsp wheat germ
> 1 tsp grated lemon rind
> 1 tbsp roated peanuts

Cut up the figs, and place them and their soaking water in the blender with the nut milk. Mix the molasses with the wheat germ and lemon rind, and add to the milk.

Blend for half a minute, then add the roasted peanuts and blend again. Eat with an orange, some satsumas, a handful of black grapes or a slice of fresh pineapple.

Calorie count: about 480.

Here are some high protein breakfasts, which will give you increased staying power all day. If protein makes you feel tense, increase the amount of carbohydrate you eat with it (see below). For a well-balanced breakfast, start off with one of the fruit juices or fruit-based starter ideas.

Kidneys on toast

Kidneys make a light protein meal, are easily digested, and also combine well with scrambled eggs, mushrooms, asparagus, and green 'extras' such as fresh parsley, watercress, mustard and cress and sprouted seeds. All of these contain chlorophyll and are good sources of magnesium. Alfalfa provides the valuable vitality nutrient octacosanol, and sprouted fenugreek seeds have a 'bucking up' effect when you are feeling exhausted.

>1 dsp safflower oil for frying
>2 lamb's kidneys or 2 large slices pig's kidney
>1 tomato
>2 mushrooms
>1 pinch sage
>Worcestershire Sauce
>medium bunch of watercress

Heat the oil in a small frying pan, add the kidneys, chopped up tomato, sliced mushrooms and sage. Cover and turn the heat down low – the meat and other ingredients will cook partly in the oil and partly in their own juices and steam. When the tomatoes and mushrooms are soft and moist, and the kidneys brown all over, remove from the pan, add a very little Worcester sauce, and eat on a slice of wholemeal toast, decorated with the watercress.

Steak tartare and alfalfa sprouts

> 3 oz/75 g fillet steak
> 1 tbsp lemon juice and 1 tsp grated rind
> salt and pepper
> 2 tbsp alfalfa sprouts

Mince the steak very finely, mix with the lemon juice and rind, and season with salt and pepper. Chop up the alfalfa sprouts, mix these in, and eat straight away.

Calorie count: about 185.

Scrambled liver with wheat germ

You can either use a small slice of raw liver for this, or save a cooked piece from a previous meal.

> small knob of margarine
> 2 oz/50 g lamb's, calf's or pig's liver, finely chopped
> 2 large eggs
> a little skimmed milk
> salt and pepper
> 1 tbsp wheat germ

Melt the margarine in a small pan, gently fry the raw liver for 5 or 6 minutes, then remove it to a plate and keep warm. Take the pan off the heat for a moment, break the eggs into the pan, mix in with the melted fat, and scramble over a low heat with a drop of skimmed milk and the seasoning. Just before the eggs are ready, chop the liver and add it and the wheat germ to the pan; stir well. Eat on or with a slice of wholemeal bread or toast.

Calorie count: about 450 without the toast.

Super-porridge (recipe on page 63) is another excellent breakfast for energy and stamina, especially when served with molasses. A pleasant variation is to add a teaspoon of grated orange peel to it, immediately before eating. Sweeten with either clear honey or a little molasses.

Alfalfa sprout and wheat germ soda bread

This energy-giving bread can be eaten with either sweet or savoury toppings, and makes good lunchtime sandwiches.

>8 oz/225 g wholewheat flour
>3 oz/75 g soya flour
>1 oz/25 g wheat germ
>1 tsp bicarbonate of soda
>1 tsp cream of tartar
>1 tsp salt
>3 heaped tbsp alfalfa sprouts
>1 dsp molasses
>buttermilk for mixing

Place the flours, wheat germ, bicarbonate of soda, cream of tartar and salt in a mixing bowl, add the buttermilk, molasses and sprouts, and mix to a moderately stiff dough. Place on a floured baking tray, and pat into a round, flattish shape, about ten inches/25 cm in diameter. Mark with a large cross in the centre. Bake for 25 to 30 minutes in an oven preheated to 220°C/425°F or gas mark 7, or until the top is golden brown. Cool on a wire rack.

Calorie count: if you cut the loaf into ten slices, each slice provides about 135 calories.

Moody muesli, mark 5

Here is a muesli with a high proportion of wheat germ to suit your extra energy needs. Eat with some plain yoghourt, and/or fresh orange juice.

>2 tbsp wheat germ
>2 tbsp porridge oats

> 1 medium banana, sliced
> 1 large orange, sliced
> 2 tbsp alfalfa sprouts
> 1 tbsp raisins
> 1 tbsp pumpkin seeds
> 2 tsp clear honey

Mix the wheat germ and oats with the sliced banana and orange. Mix in the alfalfa sprouts raisins and seeds and sweeten with the honey. This is sufficient for either one or two servings, depending upon how much yoghourt you eat with it!

Calorie count: about 835.

For pain relief, protein food with a reasonable content of tryptophan should be taken with or before carbohydrates. The scrambled eggs with liver dish above would be suitable, eaten with bread or toast. Another breakfast idea is fruit and/or fruit juice to start, followed by a slice of the alfalfa sprout and wheat germ loaf spread thickly with peanut butter. Sprinkle with pumpkin and/or sesame seeds for extra tryptophan.

Lunches

Foods rich in energy-essential nutrients are easy to turn into salads, sandwiches and soups. When two of the three food classes of pulses, nuts and grains are combined to yield all the essential amino acids, a number of the vital energy-increasing vitamins and minerals are taken in simultaneously – magnesium, iron and zinc for instance, are in many of them.

Soya bean, alfalfa and tofu salad

This is very rich in protein as it stands. If you also eat a wholewheat bread sandwich with one of the fillings suggested below, you will be boosting your stamina levels most satisfactorily.

3 oz/75 g tofu
1 clove garlic, finely chopped
salt and pepper
1 head of chicory, chopped
3 oz/75 g soya beans, cooked
2 grated carrots
6 sliced radishes
3 tbsp alfalfa sprouts
1 tbsp fresh garden herbs, mixed
2 or 3 tbsp lemony yoghourt dressing (see below)

Mash the tofu with a fork, add the chopped garlic and season with the salt and pepper. Mix well together, set on one side. In a bowl, mix the chopped chicory, soya beans, carrots and radishes and alfalfa sprouts. Break up the tofu into largish pieces and mix in with the salad vegetables. Scatter the fresh herbs on top, and pour the dressing over it.

Calorie count: about 555 without dressing.

Lemony yoghourt dressing

3 tbsp plain yoghourt
1 tbsp lemon juice
1 tsp grated lemon rind
1 dsp clear honey
1 tsp chopped fresh sage or half tsp dried sage
salt and pepper

Simply mix all the ingredients well together, and use with salad.

Calorie count: about 85.

Barley winter salad

Use pot barley for this recipe, instead of the pearl barley you put in stews and casseroles.

3 oz/75 g pot barley, cooked
3 or 4 raw Brussels sprouts, grated
4 or 5 spring onions or slices of winter onion
3 tbsp grated root vegetables, e.g. turnips, swedes, parsnips
1 grated carrot
3 oz cold, lean roast beef, chopped into ½ inch/1 cm cubes
Horseradish dressing (see below)

Drain and cool the barley, and mix it with the grated vegetables and the cold meat. Spoon on some dressing and eat this with a slice or two of wholewheat bread, or alfalfa sprout and wheatgerm soda bread, (page 141) spread with a little skimmed milk cheese.

Calorie count: about 300.

Horseradish dressing

1 tsp finely grated fresh horseradish root or 1 dsp bottled horseradish sauce
2 level tbsp soured cream
1 tsp clear honey
½ tsp paprika pepper

Calorie count: about 165.

Black-eyed bean salad with pasta and chives

This salad combines all three vegetarian ingredients – pasta (representing the grains), pulses and nuts, thus providing a wide assortment of amino acids as well as other nutrients.

2 oz/50 g black-eyed beans, cooked
2 oz/50 g wholewheat pasta shells, cooked
chunk of Chinese cabbage, chopped
1 large tomato, chopped
handful of fenugreek sprouts
1 tbsp chopped chives
1 tbsp roasted hazelnuts
2 tbsp tomato juice

Mix all the dry ingredients together, and moisten with the tomato juice, canned or from a tin of peeled tomatoes. A few drops of Tabasco sauce on this brings the flavour out very well.

Calorie count: about 310

Sandwiches

Here are some ideas for sandwich fillings which are aimed to bolster your energy reserves for the rest of the day, without making you feel bloated and sleepy. If carbohydrate taken at midday does have that effect on you, I suggest you stick to salads, fruit and fruit drinks, eating only as much of any of these as you need to keep your energy at a satisfactory level, while avoiding that unpleasant 'sated' feeling.

1 an avocado pear well mashed with a 'just' hard-boiled egg, mixed with enough plain yoghourt to moisten the filling, a little salt and pepper, and some sprouted seeds (mustard and cress, fenugreek, alfalfa).

2 crunchy peanut butter, mixed with plenty of chopped alfalfa sprouts, half a teaspoon of brewer's yeast (this needs to be amalgamated with ingredients with very strong flavours), and some low-salt vegetable yeast extract.

3 kidney pâté (page 71), mixed with a little very finely chopped raw spinach leaves and some slices of tomato.

4 prawns, with a little lemon juice and rind, and a very

little cayenne pepper, mixed with some mashed tofu.

5 a mixture of all the sprouted seeds you can find, plus a little watercress, finely shredded, and some cottage cheese.

6 some bought lemon curd (made with natural ingredients only, no artificial additives), mixed with a little extra grated lemon peel and some wheatgerm.

Spiced black-eyed bean soup

When any recipe says 2 oz/50 g of a pulse or grain, you will find it more economical to cook three or four times this quantity, and use the rest in a soup or savoury dish. Here is a recipe using the black-eyed beans that you have left over from the salad recipe above.

> 1 dsp safflower oil
> a chopped onion
> 1 tsp ground coriander
> 1 tsp ground cumin
> 6 oz/175 g cooked black-eyed beans plus their cooking stock
> 1 tsp brewer's yeast
> 5 fl oz/150 ml evaporated milk
> 1 tsp brewer's yeast
> salt and pepper

Heat the oil in a saucepan, and cook the finely chopped onion for four or five minutes over a gentle heat. Add the spices, and cook for a further five minutes, stirring occasionally. Then add the beans and their stock, and add a little more boiling water if you think there is insufficient liquid. Bring to the boil, stirring, then turn down the heat and simmer gently for ten minutes. Pour into the blender, add the brewer's yeast, liquidize, return to the saucepan, and stir in the evaporated milk. Season with a little salt and pepper. This makes enough for two or three servings.

Calorie count: about 635.

Pub Lunches

Take this opportunity to eat some meat or egg protein, if you have not included this at breakfast time. Carefully cut any fat or gristle off the meat, and eat an unbuttered wholemeal roll or bread, or some rye bread, so that you do not include any more saturated (or other) fat than you need to. Eat a large salad alongside, including as much greenery as you can – lettuce, watercress, and ordinary cress may well be available, even if you are unlikely to find sprouted alfalfa!

If you are a non-meat eater, choose hard-boiled eggs (without salad cream), some Brie, Camembert or other fairly low fat cheese (Edam and Gouda are ideal), and follow with some fresh fruit if you are still hungry.

Avoid alcohol because of its soporific effect, and choose unsweetened pure citrus fruit juices or mineral water. Although pineapple is not a 'citrus' fruit, its juice does make a refreshing drink, mixing one small bottle of it with some ice cubes in a tall tumbler, topping up with soda water, and adding a lemon slice or two on top for good measure.

Evening Meal

Occasionally, you only want a nutritious snack in the evening if you have eaten more than you are accustomed to at lunch time, or your appetite is simply at a low ebb. Beef tea is highly nutritious and energy-giving, and can be accompanied by a wholewheat roll and cheese, or followed by cheese on toast if there is still room (see the recipe for 'Boozy welsh rarebit' on page 125).

Beef tea

---

4 oz/100 g lean, juicy beef (no fat or skin)
5 fl oz/150 ml cold water
a little salt

Mince the meat, soak it for half an hour in the water to which the salt has been added, then place in a clean saucepan over a very gentle heat. *Slowly* increase the temperature, squeezing the juice out of the meat by pressing it against the sides of the pan with a wooden spoon. On no account let the liquid boil. When it reaches just below boiling point, remove from the heat and strain into a warm cup.

Calorie count: about 180.

Rapid fish supper

This is a very quick and simple method of cooking white fish, either fresh or frozen. Eat it with some mashed potato, into which you have stirred a little strong Cheddar cheese and as much chopped parsley as you like.

1 tbsp safflower or olive oil
6 spring onions or ½ a medium onion, sliced
1 crushed garlic clove
6 oz/175 g whiting, cod, plaice or other white fish
small tin tomatoes
chopped chives
or alfalfa sprouts

Heat the oil in a frying pan, add the onions and garlic, and fry very gently for 5 minutes with the lid on so that the onions cook in their juices and the steam. Add your piece of fish, and the tinned tomatoes, replace the lid, and continue to cook over a very low heat for ten to twenty minutes depending on the thickness of your fish and whether it starts off frozen. Fish is 'done' the moment its flesh loses its translucency and becomes flakeable. Sprinkle some chopped chives over the top, or a handful of alfalfa sprouts if they happen to be sitting on your window sill.

Calorie count: about 275 calories.

Stewed figs with raisins and pistachio nuts

This is a fairly effortless dessert, as you can soak the dried figs all day, cook them until soft in a little water with a piece of lemon peel in the evening, and use them, cold, the next evening. (Use the surplus, if you cook more, in a breakfast milk shake – they are very nice with chilled soya milk.)

3 or 4 cooked figs (see above)
1 tbsp raisins (these can soak with the figs once cooked)
large handful of pistachio nuts in their shells
about 2 fl oz/50 ml soured cream
1 dsp wheat germ

Mix the figs and raisins (both should be well chilled). Shell the pistachio nuts, add to the fruit, spoon some soured cream on the top and sprinkle over the wheat germ.

Calorie count: about 450

Stuffed onions

This is a delicious vegetarian dish, and simplicity itself. Just double the quantities if you are extra hungry, and eat with a tomato and chive salad, dressed with cider vinegar dressing and garnished with watercress.

1 large onion
1 heaped tbsp cooked brown rice
1 heaped tbsp grated Cheshire cheese
a little tomato juice to moisten
1 tbsp sunflower seeds
salt and pepper
Worcestershire sauce

Boil the onion until fairly soft but not completely cooked.

Remove from water, leave until cool enough to handle comfortably, then cut off its top and scoop out some of its inside. Chop this finely, and mix with the rice, grated cheese, a little tomato juice and the seeds. Add a little salt and pepper and a drop or two of Worcestershire sauce. Stuff this, using a teaspoon, back into the onion, piling it up well. Replace the lid, cover it with greaseproof paper, and bake it for half an hour at 190° C/375° or gas mark 5. Remove the paper for the last ten minutes to allow the onion to brown.

Calorie count: about 350.

Fresh fruit salad with cashew nut cream

Cashew nut cream (sometimes called butter) can be bought at, or ordered through, most health food shops. Vegans often use it as a substitute for cream – as do many other enthusiasts – since its taste is sweet and rich, and goes perfectly with both fresh and canned fruit.

> handful of fresh cherries
> a few seedless grapes
> large sliced orange
> 6 fresh strawberries
> a sliced peach
> 2 tbsp cashew nut cream

Remove the stones from the cherries if you feel you must (essential if you are serving this to a young child). Mix the cherries with the grapes, orange, strawberries and peach, and eat with the cashew nut cream on top.

You can make your own nut cream from cashew or any other nuts, by liquidizing them in a blender and adding a very little water and a squeeze of lemon juice, until you have got it to the consistency you like. However, I do think the commercially prepared nut creams have the edge over homemade ones, for some reason.

Calorie count: 155 without the nut cream, 310 with the nut cream, using 1 oz/25 g of shelled cashew nuts.

Here is a dinner party menu with enough tryptophan for anyone wanting to maintain a good supply (for combatting aches and pains, sleeping soundly etc.) and plenty of energy-supplying nutrients to keep you chatting intelligently for as long as your guests want to stay (even if you have cooked dinner unaided, after a tiring day).

Kidney soup

8 oz/225 g calves' or lambs' kidneys
3 oz/75 g lean beef
1 oz/25g margarine
2 small onions, finely chopped
½ oz/15 g wholewheat flour
2 pints/1.25 l vegetable or chicken stock
salt and pepper
½ tsp mace
large pinches of thyme, sage, rosemary
1 dsp Worcestershire sauce

Wash the kidneys, remove the membranes, and mince them together with the lean beef. Melt nearly all the margarine in a saucepan, add the meats and fry until well browned. Remove them to a plate, add the rest of the margarine, and fry the onions. Stir in the flour and cook for two or three minutes until evenly browned. Return the meats to the saucepan, add stock, seasoning, and herbs, and the Worcestershire sauce. Simmer for about an hour and a half, until the meat is tender. Liquidize thoroughly, and serve with small cubed croutons of wholewheat bread over which you have sprinkled a very little Tabasco sauce.

Excelsior layered salad

This is a special salad, and deserves to be made in the height of the summer season when all the vegetables are at their best. Serve it with baked potatoes in their jackets, and treat yourself and your guests to some unsalted butter to spread on the crispy jackets at the end.

---

1 crisp Cos lettuce
1 head of chicory
12–16 oz/350–450 g ripe tomatoes
2 or 3 dozen spring onions
1 large red and 1 large yellow pepper
best part of a head of celery (save outside stalks for soup)
mustard and cress, sprouted fenugreek, sprouted alfalfa
1 bunch watercress
1 medium to large beetroot, fresh boiled
24 to 30 firm, bright red radishes
12 oz/350 g Roulé or Boursin cheese
12 oz/350 g sliced chicken breast
4 hard-boiled eggs
2 avocado pears, skinned and sliced lengthways
1 dozen large black olives

You need either a very deep glass dish for this salad, so that you can arrange the ingredients in layers and the pretty effect can then be seen, or a large china meat dish, on which you can lay everything out to look its best.

If you use the glass dish, start if you like with the coarsely shredded lettuce, and then arrange alternate layers of salad vegetables and egg, cheese and chicken, inventing a pattern of contrasting colours. In this way, the whites, yellows and greens show vividly against the reds and purples.

I usually spread the cheese in a layer on the top, decorating it with carefully arranged slices of avocado pear, between which I arrange large black olives. Whatever you do, do not end with the chicken slices and leave the salad on the kitchen table as I did the first time I made it. Mr Shastri, my Persian cat, was too strongly tempted and leapt onto the kitchen table, knocking the salad for six!

This is a good reminder that the salad should be well chilled in the fridge, anyway, before serving!

Blackcurrant summer pudding

Blackcurrants are brimming over with goodness – vitamin C to be precise, and the rosehip syrup adds a little 'extra' to the flavour, while adding considerably to the vitamin C content.

1 lb/450 g fresh blackcurrants
water
brown sugar or clear honey to taste
several slices of stale wholewheat bread (the actual quantity depends upon the size of the dish, likely appetite of guests etc.)
10 fl oz/300 ml whipping cream
1 dsp runny honey
half tsp cinnamon

Stew the currants with a very little water and sugar or honey to taste, until they are tender. Line a dessert dish with slices of the bread (you can cut them fairly thick), and pour the fruit on top, alternating it with slices of bread, and ending with bread. Cover this with a plate, and place a heavy weight on top (e.g. a large tin of fruit, juice or vegetables, or a glass jar full of pulses). Leave this for several hours, in the refrigerator, serve with whipping cream, into which you have stirred a dessertspoonful of runny honey and some powdered cinnamon.

Boost Your Sexual Vigour

Although more men than women tend to worry about having a low sex drive, loss of interest in lovemaking affects the two sexes equally. It is generally more apparent in men, since a diminished desire for sexual fulfilment is frequently accompanied by poor 'performance', i.e. the inability to obtain or sustain an erection, and/or the inability to reach orgasm. Women, on the other hand, traditionally although not factually, are less interested in sex anyway, and can either get away with admitting to 'not feeling like it', or put up with it, faking the occasional orgasm so as not to appear frigid.

There is no doubt that a great deal of anxiety and distress is generated by loss of libido (sexual interest). This can be due to a very large number of both physical and psychological health problems, which may need diagnosis and treatment before sexual activity can improve. Sometimes, simply allaying anxiety on the subject can have a highly beneficial effect, and this is where sexual therapy and counselling can prove very useful. In many people, however, lack of arousal can be helped by nutritional means.

Which Foods?

Physical and mental fatigue, anxiety, prolonged stress and depression are major factors in depleting sexual interest and activity. All these conditions tend to lower sex drive, and the change to a high raw wholefood way of eating can have highly beneficial effects. In addition, certain specific nutrients have been identified as helping to increase sexual interest and the likelihood of satisfaction.

Vitamin E is believed to increase fertility in both men and women, and it is certain that it helps muscles, nerves and glands throughout the body to perform normally. Some people who take this vitamin in supplementary form, feel sure that it increases their sex drive, although this has not so far been proved.

Zinc has long been believed to play an important role in the control of sexual activity and initial arousal. A deficiency of zinc is often found in men suffering from impotence and in people of both sexes complaining of lack of sexual desire. It is also known to be indispensable for penile erection, and high zinc foods can have a pleasing effect upon a problem that worries many of us at one time or another. It is interesting that oysters, believed for centuries to possess aphrodisiac properties, are very rich in zinc.

The main food sources of both vitamin E and zinc are shown in the table on pages 196–200.

Protein is needed for all physical activities, and sex is one of the most energetic forms of physical exercise.

Twenty minutes of passionate lovemaking have been found to burn up 200 calories. This compares favourably with twenty minutes of tennis, which only burn up 140 calories. Sex even holds its own against the high-energy activity of skipping which, for someone weighing 150 pounds and turning the rope 120 – 140 times a minute, utilizes 240 calories in a twenty-minute period. In any case, except in rare circumstances neither of these two forms of physical exercise holds a candle to lovemaking, in terms of sheer enjoyment.

A full complement of the essential amino acids is therefore vital, but in the context of sexual activity, the amino acid **histidine** seems to be particularly important. The ability to reach orgasm, either through lovemaking or through masturbation, is directly related to the level of histamine in the tissues, and it is from histidine that histamine is made. Low histamine women find it difficult to climax, and low histamine men often find problems with ejaculation although they may be able to get an erection. An increasing dietary intake of histidine may very well increase your sexual arousal level. To enable histidine to have this effect, pyridoxine (vitamin B6) and niacin (B3) are necessary. (Foods containing them are shown in the table on pages 196-200).

Histidine-rich foods include dried, non-fat milk, turkey, veal, peanuts and peanut butter, cottage cheese, chicken and eggs (whole).

Arginine is another amino acid thought to improve sexual functions. It is a precursor to the nitrogen-containing substance spermine found in semen, and seems especially relevant to male arousal and activity. It is found in dried, non-fat milk, beef, turkey, chicken, haddock, halibut, peanuts and peanut butter, pecan nuts, walnuts, shredded wheat and red kidney beans. Arginine requires a good supply of pyridoxine to have full effect.

Phenylalanine has also been found to increase interest in sex, as well as producing a feeling of greater alertness. It also has an antidepressant effect twenty-four to forty-eight hours after being taken. Perhaps this combination of properties, make this amino acid the perfect natural sexual stimulator! Foods containing it have already been discussed on page 29.

NB In the recipe section various herbs, spices and herbal teas are mentioned as possibly possessing aphrodisiac properties, and are included wherever relevant. I am not listing them here, as very little is known about them biochemically, which means that practically all the information about them is legendary and/or anecdotal.

There is every reason to eat foods that increase sexual vigour, whether one feels that one's energies are flagging in that direction or not! For one thing, the 'high raw' aspect of the foods concerned is extremely beneficial in many respects to everyone. For another, the actual foods serve a multititude of biochemical purposes throughout the body, besides that of increasing sexual interest and arousal capacity. Even if you have no current sexual partner, and no intention of acquiring one in the foreseeable future, it is just as well to be as healthy as possible in every way, instead of firing on only three out of four cylinders!

Recipes

Breakfast

Most herbal preparations made from plants with reputed aphrodisiac properties exert their effect shortly after they are drunk. If you especially want to feel sexually vigorous first thing in the morning, then try a cup of basil tea, made from the ordinary basil herb growing in your garden or kept in its dried form in your kitchen. Basil is believed by Italian tradition to increase the size of the penis, and is used in New Mexico as a traditional love potion.

Basil tea

Infuse the herb according to the method described for Lemon balm tea, page 31. If you do decide to sweeten it, try using a teaspoon of molasses instead of honey, as this supplies vitamin B 6.

Raspberry leaf tea

This herbal tea (you can also buy raspberry leaf tablets) is recommended as an aid to easy childbirth, because it tones up all the muscles of the female reproductive system. This would seem a good reason for taking it if you are a woman, even if you are not pregnant. (If you are, it is always best to consult a qualified medical practitioner or herbal specialist, if you intend to take any herbal preparations of any type whatever.)

Raspberry leaf tea is made in the same way as the other herbal teas I have mentioned.

Ginseng has a reputation for increasing sexual performance, but a considerable amount of controversy exists about whether it in fact does so. Siberian Ginseng, on the other hand, a distant cousin of the ordinary type, is a more powerful herb in every sense. Basically, it increases endurance as well as accelerating one's recovery period following any bout of strenuous exercise, and can be taken as a restorative tea for this purpose.

Fresh juices

Practically any fresh fruit and vegetables juices will be beneficial to you, since they are the essence of raw goodness. However, one specifically recommended by Bridget Amies 'to promote strength and health' comprises 4 fl oz/ 100 ml each of carrot and grape juice, mixed with one teaspoon of radish juice, taken slowly before meals.

Here is one that is extra rich in vitamin E:

>broccoli – enough to make 5 fl oz/150 ml
>Brussels sprouts – enough to make an equal quantity

Drink this at breakfast time with a teaspoon of wheat germ stirred in.

Bridget Amies recommends 4 fl oz/100 ml taken four times a day, of the following juice combination, for rejuvenation – equal parts of celery and cabbage juice, in to which you stir one tablespoon of either lemon, orange or grapefruit juice.

Here is another melon-based fruit starter (or whole breakfast if you are in a tearing hurry). One of the reasons melon features so often in these breakfast recipes generally, is that it is an excellent source of vitamin B 6.

Crunchy melon starter

>6 oz/175 g slice of melon, preferably canteloup
>1 tbsp pumpkin seeds
>1 tbsp roasted peanuts
>2 tsp molasses
>2 tsp wheat germ
>1 tsp dried yeast (optional)

Scrape the flesh from the melon skin having discarded the seeds. Mix the flesh, chopped roughly, with the rest of the ingredients, stirring it round well so that the dry ingredients get thoroughly coated with the melon juice. Add a teaspoon of dried yeast if you like the taste.

Calorie count: about 450.

As with Momento melon (page 33) you can liquidize all these ingredients in the blender together with 15 fl oz/450 ml of skimmed milk or soya milk, and drink it as a milk shake. The calorie count would be 600 using skimmed milk, and 630 using soya milk.

Wheat germ is such a splendid source of vitamin E and zinc, as also are eggs, that combining them in a breakfast drink is a very good idea for helping to increase (over a period of time!) your sexual prowess.

Egg enhancer

10 fl oz/300 ml peanut milk (see page 34), made using
1 oz/25 g nuts
1 large egg
1 tbsp rosehip syrup
1 tbsp wheat germ
1 dsp soured cream
1 tbsp pumpkin seeds

Liquidize the nut milk, egg, syrup, and wheat germ for about a minute. Either use very cold nut milk, or pour into a glass with three or four ice cubes. Spoon the soured cream on the top, and scatter the pumpkin seeds on the blob of cream.

Calorie count: about 545.

Here is a protein breakfast which includes turkey, rich in histidine.

East turkey scramble

3 oz/175 g turkey breast, cooked
2 eggs
skimmed milk to mix
small knob of margarine
1 tsp wheat germ
¼ tsp basil
1 tbsp alfalfa sprouts
salt and pepper

Chop up the turkey breast finely, scramble the eggs in a

pan with the milk and margarine, then mix in the wheat germ, basil and sprouts. Season, and eat straight away.

Calorie count: about 400.

Breakfast liver grill

Liver for breakfast may sound strange, but if you happen to like it very much and enjoy cooked breakfasts anyway, there is every reason why you should eat it in place of a conventional 'fry'.

> 2 or 3 thin slices of calves' liver
> 3 or 4 large mushrooms
> 2 or 3 tomatoes
> a little safflower oil
> salt and pepper
> ¼ tsp basil
> 1 tsp pumpkin seeds

Brush the liver slices, mushrooms and tomatoes with the oil, season lightly and add the basil. Grill until cooked, then eat with the pumpkin seeds scattered on top.

Calorie count: about 310.

A slice of oatmeal bread would go well with either of these dishes (see below). Alternatively, you might like to try a slice of wholemeal scone, with added soya flour, wheat germ, pumpkin seeds and oats. (Oat extract is often included in herbal preparations designed to improve sexual vigour. Oats are not an aphrodisiac, but they calm tense nerves and improve muscle tone.)

Oatmeal bread

> 5 oz/150 g wholemeal flour
> 1 oz/25 g soya flour
> pinch of salt
> 1 oz/25 g oatmeal

      1 tbsp wheat germ
      1 tsp baking powder
      1 oz/25 g margarine
      2 tbsp pumpkin seeds
      6 fl oz/175 ml skimmed milk

Put the flours, salt, oatmeal and wheat germ into a bowl with the baking powder. Add the margarine, cut it through the dry ingredients with a knife, then rub the small pieces in until the mixture resembles fine breadcrumbs. Add the seeds and the milk and mix to a soft dough. Knead it gently for about three minutes, then place it on a floured baking tray and pat it into the shape of a flat, rounded loaf, about 1 inch/2.5 cm thick. Mark into eight wedge-shaped slices by scoring the top with a sharp knife. Brush the top with a little skimmed milk and bake it in an oven preheated to 230°C/450°F or gas mark 8 for about fifteen minutes or until golden brown.

Calorie count: about 160 per slice.

Moody muesli, mark 6

Both oatmeal and peanuts supply niacin, necessary for the sexual stimulatory effects of histidine.

      2 tbsp porridge oats
      1 tbsp whole wheat flakes
      1 tbsp toasted sesame seeds
      1 tbsp pumpkin seeds
      1 tbsp wheat germ
      1 tbsp roasted peanuts
      2 tbsp raisins
      freshly squeezed orange juice to moisten well

Mix all the ingredients and leave them to soak overnight in the orange juice. This recipe is enough for two servings.

Calorie count: about 435 per serving.

Lunch

Because of the close relationship between fresh raw vegetables, fruit, seeds and nuts, and an increase in both general and sexual vigour, you should definitely aim to include a large salad in your daily meals. Here are some salad ideas.

Butter bean, spinach and anchovy salad

3 spring onions
3 medium tomatoes
a handful of raw spinach, washed and chopped roughly
2 oz/50 g butter beans, cooked
1 tbsp chopped parsley
a few anchovy fillets
basil vinaigrette (see below)

Chop the onions and tomatoes, mix with the spinach, butter beans, parsley, and anchovy fillets drained of their oil. How many you include depends on how much you like anchovies – about eight 'strips' seem the right amount to me. Add as much of the dressing as you like, just before eating, accompanied by some of the breakfast scone (page 160) or wholewheat bread.

Calorie count: about 110.

Basil vinaigrette

3 tbsp safflower oil
1 tbsp cider vinegar
salt and pepper
pinch of brown sugar
1 tsp fresh basil or half tsp dried

Mix or blend everything together.

Calorie count: about 370.

Turkey, bulgur wheat and endive salad

The brown meat of turkey, more flavoursome than breast meat, goes better in this salad. One large drumstick provides about the right quantity.

about 4 oz/100 g turkey
basil mayonnaise (see below)
2 oz/50 g bulgur wheat, soaked
3 or 4 small tomatoes, chopped
3 or 4 spring onions
a handful of watercress

Cut the turkey into biggish pieces and coat with the mayonnaise. Mix in the bulgur wheat, tomatoes and spring onions, and cut or tear the watercress up roughly. If you are taking this as a packed lunch, add the watercress just before eating the salad, or eat it separately.

Calorie count: about 400 without the mayonnaise.

Basil mayonnaise

Make this in the blender, it is by far the quickest way.

1 whole egg
1 tbsp lemon juice
½ tsp brown sugar
1 dsp fresh basil or 1 tsp dried
salt and pepper to taste
5 fl oz/150 ml safflower or olive oil

Place all the ingredients except the oil in the blender. Remove the central cap and switch on. Pour the oil in a very thin stream into the goblet through the centre of the lid, until the desired consistency is reached (you cannot always tell, while it is blending, how thick the mixture is, so stop the blending every few moments to check it). Cup your hand over the opening initially, until the blades are covered by the mixture, to avoid being splashed! All the ingredients must be at room temperature.

Calorie count: 1,340.

Pasta salad with shrimps

This salad is high in vitamin E, which is provided by the broccoli, wholewheat pasta, wheat germ, eggs and the oil in the mayonnaise. The shrimps give you tryptophan and phenylalanine.

> 3 oz/75 g wholewheat pasta spirals, cooked
> 1 dsp wheat germ
> basil mayonnaise (see previous recipe)
> 3 oz/75 g broccoli heads
> 3 oz/75 g peeled shrimps
> 1 large hard-boiled egg
> large handful of sprouting seeds (alfalfa, preferably)

Rinse the cooked pasta well after cooking and drain. Mix the wheatgerm into the mayonnaise and stir into the pasta to coat well. Plunge the broccoli into boiling water for about 3 minutes, remove, drain and cool. Mix it in with the pasta, and add the shrimps, the egg, cut into large chunks, and the sprouting seeds. Add a little more of the mayonnaise if you like and stir in well.

Calorie count: about 410, without the mayonnaise.

Wholewheat bread (try granary) is nice with all of the above salads. Try it spread with a little low fat soft cheese to make the following sandwiches.

Sandwich fillings

1 a slice of cold roast veal, trimmed of any fat or gristle, with some thinly sliced beetroot, and chopped curly endive leaves (add a little mayonnaise if you like).

2 cold cooked butter beans, drained, mashed to a paste with a finely chopped tomato, a very little olive oil and one small chopped garlic clove.

3 tahini, mixed with half its own volume of clear honey, and some chopped walnuts and pumpkin seeds.

4 avocado pear, mashed with a little lemon juice and salt and pepper, and mixed with whole peeled prawns.

5 cottage cheese, mixed with a little parmesan and some freshly ground black pepper, and thin slices of cucumber.

6 a hard-boiled egg (preferably not boiled too hard), chopped and mixed with basil mayonnaise (page 163) and either mustard and cress or other sprouting seeds.

Watercress soup

This is delicious eaten either hot with wholemeal bread or any of the above sandwiches, on a cold day, or icy cold in summer.

8 oz/225 g cooked potatoes
1 large bunch watercress
15 fl oz/450 ml whole milk
salt and pepper
1 tbsp melted butter
chopped parsley

Place the potatoes in a blender with a little of the water in which they were cooked, and blend until smooth. Switch off, add the washed watercress and blend again, either until the soup is entirely smooth, or until the watercress has been roughly chopped. Return to the saucepan, add the milk, and bring to simmering point. Remove from heat, season to taste and stir in the melted butter just before serving. Sprinkle with chopped parsley.

Calorie count: about 580.

Pub Lunch

High protein lunches, preferably in salad form, are your obvious choice. Chicken, turkey, veal, cottage cheese and eggs all provide histidine, and lamb is rich in zinc. Eggs provide both of these nutrients, as well as many others, and in their hard-boiled form are probably your best choice, combined with dark green leafy vegetables.

A word about alcohol. Avoid drinking at lunchtime if you are anxious to feel sexually vigorous later in the day. A little alcohol is an excellent thing taken with a meal when you want to feel relaxed and witty, but too much really does 'increase desire while taking away performance'! The last thing you want by the time the evening comes is to feel even remotely hung over.

Evening Meal

This recipe combines veal (for the histidine it provides) with low fat soft cheese which provides phenylalanine, and wheat germ giving zinc and vitamin E.

Veal with soft cheese

1 oz/25 g low fat soft cheese
½ tsp dried basil or 1 tsp fresh
1 × 6 oz/175 g veal escalope
1 heaped tbsp seasoned flour
small egg, beaten
2 oz/50 g dry wholewheat breadcrumbs
2 tbsp safflower oil
watercress to garnish
½ fresh lemon

Mix the soft cheese with the basil and spread it over both sides of the escalope. Coat it with the seasoned flour, dip it into the egg to moisten it all over, then press the breadcrumbs on all over it. Chill in the refrigerator for an hour at least.

Heat the oil in a frying pan, and fry the escalope on

both sides until cooked through – between five and ten minutes. Garnish with the watercress and lemon. If you feel like eating a salad with your veal, I can recommend blanched cauliflower florets, cooled slightly, mixed with some freshly cooked chopped beetroot, and dressed with a garlicky vinaigrette.

Calorie count: about 420.

Banana custard

Bananas are believed by some people to have certain aphrodisiac qualities. It just depends whether they work for you. Certainly nutmeg has long had a reputation for producing and increasing sexual arousal.

1 large banana
10 fl oz/300 ml skimmed milk
2 eggs
1 heaped tbsp brown sugar
1 level tsp ground nutmeg

Slice the banana thickly, and place in a dish. To make the custard, bring the milk only just to boiling point, let the temperature decrease slightly. Beat the eggs with the sugar in a small bowl, pour on the hot milk, stirring well and return this to the saucepan. Add the nutmeg and reheat gently, stirring, until the mixture has thickened, and coat the back of a wooden spoon. Do not let it boil or it will curdle. Pour over the banana and serve either warm or chilled.

Calorie count: about 430.

Grilled trout with nutty potatoes

Trout always sound rather 'dinner partyish', but there is no reason why you shouldn't eat them for an ordinary midweek supper. They provide phenylalanine, as do the nuts.

1 medium trout, fresh or frozen and thawed
a little safflower oil
5 or 6 medium potatoes
a little skimmed milk
little black pepper
grating of nutmeg
1 tbsp each of shelled Brazil nuts, walnuts, roasted almonds
fresh lemon slices
small bunch watercress

Brush the trout over with the oil, and grill gently. Meanwhile, cook the potatoes in some salted water, drain, and mash with the skimmed milk. Season with a little black pepper and some nutmeg. Grind up the nuts in a blender or nutmill, and stir them into the mashed potato, adding a little extra milk if the mixture gets too stiff. Spoon small pyramids of the mixture on to a lightly greased baking tray, and bake them in a fairly hot oven (190°C/375°F or gas mark 5) for about twenty minutes or until they are golden brown. Serve with the trout, garnished with the lemon and watercress. This is nice with some puréed sprouts, or spinach.

Calorie count: about 640.

Peaches with strawberry sauce

1 large fresh peach
5 oz/150 g fresh strawberries, hulled
about 5 fl oz/150 ml water
1 tbsp fresh lemon juice
1 heaped tsp cornflour blended with 1 tbsp water
brown sugar to sweeten

Slice the peach into a small dish. Blend the strawberries, with the water, add the lemon juice and heat gently until just boiling. Stir in the blended cornflour, and simmer, stirring, until the mixture thickens. Stir in the sugar, then pour over the sliced peach and eat either warm as it is, or chilled.

Calorie count: about 110.

Here is a vegetarian recipe that is really quick and simplicity itself. It serves its purpose best when you face what may be a fairly energetic evening and feel too exhausted by the day's events to bother with cooking anything complicated.

Easiest spaghetti

4 oz/100 g wholewheat spaghetti (raw weight)
1 tbsp olive oil
1 or 2 garlic cloves, chopped
2 tbsp grated parmesan cheese
plenty of black pepper
grated nutmeg
1 large handful of bean sprouts or other sprouted seeds

Cook the spaghetti in plenty of slightly salted boiling water. Rinse, drain well, and mix in the olive oil, garlic cloves, grated parmesan, black pepper and nutmeg. Just before serving, mix in the sprouted seeds.

Calorie Count: about 700.

A light, juicy salad goes well with this.

Tomato and green pepper salad

½ large green pepper
several slices of a large beef tomato
2 inch/5 cm length of unpeeled cucumber
6 or 7 spring onions
malt vinegar
black pepper

Deseed the pepper and remove the white membranes. Chop everything up roughly into large chunks, cutting the vegetables over the dish in which you are going to serve them so that none of the juice is lost. A few spots of malt vinegar and a grinding of black pepper are the only essential accompaniments. A piece of fresh fruit is an excellent way of rounding off this meal.

Calorie count: about 25.

Here is a menu for entertaining at a dinner party which is strictly *à deux*. Set the table prettily, light the candles and let the brain nutrients do their best for you and your guest!

Oysters for starters

Oysters are expensive and, while no clinical trials have been carried out, to my knowledge, to test their aphrodisiac qualities, I really do not think that foods become legendary for possessing certain properties without a very good reason! As I mentioned earlier, they do have a very high content of zinc

6 fresh oysters each

grated nutmeg

a little watercress to garnish

lemon quarters

Open the oysters, using an oyster knife, or get your fishmonger to open them for you. Place the shells containing the fish on a bed of crushed ice in a soup plate. Grate some fresh nutmeg over them, and serve garnished with the watercress, placing two lemon quarters in the centre of the oysters.

Serve with very thinly sliced wholewheat bread and real butter, and put out finger bowls with flower petals floating on the surface to complete the effect. Do not forget table napkins!

Calorie count: 40 calories each serving.

Loin of veal, with herb and garlic stuffing

It may seem a travesty of culinary art, to serve a delicately flavoured meat like veal with a stuffing of powerful herbs and garlic. However, the veal serves two purposes, known only to yourself as the cook. It is rich in the amino acid histidine, which is important for sexual arousal, and it is also the vehicle of the potent stuffing, rich with herbs and fenugreek whose aphrodisiac qualities are renowned, at least by hearsay.

> 4 lb/2 kg loin of veal, boned and trimmed
> salt and pepper
> grated nutmeg
> herb and garlic stuffing (see below)
> 1 tbsp grated lemon peel
> 1 oz/25 g margarine

Lay out the veal, fat side down, and season well with salt, pepper and a little nutmeg. Spread the stuffing and lemon peel over the meat, roll it up and tie it with string at one inch intervals. Dot its surface with the margarine, and roast in a fairly hot oven (190°C/375° F or gas mark 5) for between two and two and three quarter hours until the veal is cooked through.

Serve this with slices of the stuffing, buttered cabbage (cabbage is also reputed to have aphrodisiac qualities), plain boiled potatoes and a side salad of sliced fresh tomatoes (also called 'Love Apples'), dressed only in their own juice, some fresh or dried basil, and a little salt.

Calorie count: without the stuffing and accompaniments, the veal accounts for about 150 calories per 4 oz/100 g serving.

Herb and garlic stuffing

> 2 medium onions, chopped
> 3 oz/75 g fresh wholewheat breadcrumbs

½ tsp each of the following dried herbs or 1 tsp fresh (more if you dare!) star anise (from Chinese supermarkets), basil, mint, rosemary, savory, sage.
1 heaped tbsp sprouted fenugreek seeds
2 large garlic cloves, chopped
1½ oz/35 g margarine
salt and pepper
1 egg, beaten

Cook the onions until fairly tender. Drain, cut them up and mix them with the breadcrumbs, herbs, fenugreek sprouts, garlic and margarine, which you have cut up into small pieces. Season with salt and pepper, and mix well together. Bind the mixture with the egg, and if it seems too dry, moisten with a very little boiling water.

NB You will only find star anise in a dried seedpod form. Grind one or two of the dried seedpods up in a coffee grinder or blender and add half a teaspoon to the stuffing.

Calorie count: about 640 for the stuffing as a whole.

Aphrodite's dream

Most men have a sweet tooth at heart, so to speak, and so do nearly all women. Try this dessert to round off your dinner *à deux*.

2 fresh peaches or 2 canned whole peaches
2 fresh or canned green figs
12 fresh or frozen strawberries
2 tbsp canned lychees with juice or 8 fresh, peeled lychees
2 passion fruit
2 heaped tbsp pumpkin seeds
4 tbsp Cinzano Bianco

Slice the peaches, and the figs, letting all the juice run into two dishes. Chop the strawberries into large pieces, and add, together with the fresh or canned lychees. Cut open the passion fruit, and spoon out their flesh and juice into the mixture. Scatter the pumpkin seeds over the fruit, and spoon 2 tablespoons of Cinzano Bianco over each dish. Serve with almond nut cream (see page 150).

Calorie count: without nut cream, about 320 per serving. With 1 tbsp nut cream apiece, about 500 calories per serving.

Put an End to Feminine Problems

The main women's health problems that can benefit from the right choice of foods, include painful periods (dysmenorrhoea), PMS and the menopause. They are included in this book because all these can be accompanied by profound emotional changes and mood problems.

PMS

This has already been mentioned in connection with the irritability and tension that earned it its old name PMT (premenstrual tension). This is the collection of symptoms and signs that affect many girls and women for anything between two and fourteen days prior to their menstrual periods.

Some women, usually teenagers and young women in their twenties, get off lightly, and notice minimal changes during their premenstrual phase. Fifty per cent of women get enough discomfort to make them either buy over-the-counter pain killers or herbal remedies, or to ask their doctor for a prescription. The physical symptoms are mainly related to fluid retention, and include weight gain, bloatedness, tender breasts, headaches, muscular aches and pains, and food and drink cravings.

The mood changes and emotional symptoms are often more troublesome than the physical ones, and include great irritability, depression, irrational anger, sometimes accompanied by actual violent aggression, and tearfulness.

Prescriptions for pain killers and diuretic drugs are a common form of treatment. The contraceptive pill is also prescribed for PMS by some doctors. Other treatments include progesterone therapy, as it was once thought that a low progesterone level accounted for PMS symptoms in many women.

A shortage of the essential fatty acid GLA is now believed to be a far more widely spread cause. Low GLA levels affect the manufacturers of hormone-like substances called prostaglandins, that control the minute-by-minute functioning of the cells throughout our bodies.

GLA is manufactured in the body from cis-linoleic acid in the diet. Some of the most important factors that prevent our converting dietary cis-linoleic acid into GLA, include the ageing process, viral infections, diabetes, the effects of radiation and excessive amounts of stress. Others are too much saturated fat and cholesterol in the diet, and the presence of trans-linoleic acid, into which the useful cis- form of this fatty acid is converted by industrial processes used in making margarine from vegetable oils.

Which Foods?

Since tension and irritability are such frequent PMS problems, experiment with your carbohydrate intake. If taking a carbohydrate-rich meal early in the day makes you feel sleepy and unable to concentrate, then you may find that smaller amounts will make you feel more relaxed without your concentration and alertness becoming impaired.

Evening primrose oil (Efamol) will supplement GLA levels in the body. Helpful vitamins and minerals in PMS include, in particular, vitamins B6, C and E; and magnesium and zinc. Natural food supplies of these nutrients are shown in the table on page 196–200.

Period Pain

The two commonest period problems are painful periods and irregularity. Both affect teenage girls more often than older women, and are often considerably relieved after the birth of the first baby. The pain experienced once a period has started can be far more severe than non-sufferers imagine. Once, fainting attacks during periods were related unquestioningly to emotional unbalance, and the pain itself to a dread of sexual development and the approach of full womanhood.

If these were ever among the causes of bad period pain, it is highly unlikely that they are now, in any but the most exceptional cases. The pain is caused by the muscular cramp attacks that happen in the womb (uterus) wall, and these hurt just as much as cramp anywhere else. The cause of the pain in the first place, is probably the presence of 'unhelpful' prostaglandins made in the wall of the womb in high amounts in period pain sufferers.

Irregularities of the menstrual cycle normally sort themselves out. Very heavy bleeding, or unusually severe pain, nausea or fainting attacks should be discussed with your doctor. Natural means do exist, though, that will help you control the pain, and maybe relieve it altogether, especially if you combine the healthy diet approach with some daily exercise and an hour or so of relaxation.

Which Foods?

Try tryptophan-rich foods, and a carbohydrate-rich meal several hours afterwards to enable the tryptophan to enter the brain. This should help control the pain, and ease feelings of anxiety, tension or depression many women feel for the first day or so of their periods (i.e. 'period blues'). The vitamins and minerals of special use to you if you suffer from painful periods are the B complex vitamins, especially B12, folic acid; and calcium and magnesium.

Many women find that they tend to become constipated just before and during their periods. Eating complex, unrefined carbohydrates which have a high fibre content should help you to steer clear of this problem. Exercise is also a great help.

The Menopause

Most women are aware of the problems that the menopause can entail, and dread the onset of hot flushes, painful intercourse and irritability long before they reach menopausal age. Certainly, this time can be traumatic if you allow it to be, since it represents the end of the child-bearing years and therefore – many women feel – the onset of old age.

It is, however, possible to sail through the 'change of life' with minimum discomfort and one of the best ways of doing so is by means of a balanced, wholefood diet that provides optimally for your nutritional needs.

The reason for the vaginal soreness, hot flushes, tension, depression, and emotional outbursts some women experience, is the reduced output of oestrogen by the ovaries. This also causes the increased loss of calcium from the bones (osteoporosis), making them more brittle and inclined to fracture.

Which Foods?

Eating a wholefood diet with a high raw content will help combat the lethargy and poor concentration many menopausal women complain of. Large salads of fresh raw vegetables and fruit, with seeds, nuts and pulses, give a feeling of vitality without increasing your weight. Including plenty of this type of food, together with sufficient complex carbohydrate to fill you up, should ensure that you do not put on weight due to between-meal nibbling, and that you are obtaining the vitamins and minerals most useful to you at this time.

As at any other time in your life, you always need your full complement of nutrients. It is worth labouring this point here because, if you have not eaten a nutritionally adequate diet in the past, the menopause is an excellent time to start. Pay special attention to calcium-rich foods, and include some magnesium-rich ones daily to balance your calcium intake. This, combined with adequate exercise, will help to protect you from osteoporotic bone thinning.

Vitamin E is renowned for its ability to combat hot flushes. Choose foods rich in this nutrient, and add a natural supplement should you feel your diet only partly solves the problem. The same goes for your mineral intake – take a calcium and magnesium supplement if you cannot include a daily amount of calcium-rich food in your meals.

Remember, too, the 'anti-stress' properties of vitamin C; and those of the B complex vitamins. Take adequate amounts of vitamin A foods, too, as these help to keep mucous membranes in a healthy, youthful state.

Recipes

Breakfasts

You need a drink as soon as you wake that will stimulate you into full appreciation of the day's potential beauty, without making you feel thoroughly on edge at the thought of facing all it has to offer.

Lemon balm tea is an obvious choice, as are chamomile, raspberry leaf and apple tea. (See page 31 for the recipe). Others I am confident in recommending are teas made by *Salus*, such as the fruity and aromatic 'Sunrise' Aroma Tea, designed to make you feel alert and ready to face the day, and Paradise Vitamin C Fruit Aroma Tea, that combines the natural vitamin C content of the Acerola Cherry with tropical fruit.

Fresh juices

The following juice drink is specifically designed to relieve menstrual pain:

> 2 fl oz/50 ml each of raspberry, blackberry and raisin juice

To get juice from raisins, soak them first in boiling water, and juice them with their soak water.

Irregular menstrual periods are said to be helped by celery, parsley and pineapple juice. Either juice some fresh pineapple or buy some unsweetened, in a carton or can – try 5 fl oz/150 ml every morning. If you want to try the vegetable juice, make about 5 fl oz/150 ml of celery juice and include a medium handful of fresh parsley with the celery sticks.

As I pointed out earlier in this book, mood reaction to carbohydrate and protein foods varies so much from one individual to another, that your best advice is to try out different food types at different times during the day to check how you are affected personally. If period pains and/or immense tension and irritability are your problems, then a breakfast based on carbohydrate may well be best for you because of the effects of the tryptophan that would thereby be released across your blood brain barrier.

(This does of course depend upon there being some tryptophan available along with other amino acids in your bloodstream, in the first place. If you want to try this approach at breakfast time, make sure that you include the full complement of essential amino acids by eating first class protein or the appropriate vegetarian food combinations, for your evening meal the night before.)

However, if carbohydrates make you feel drowsy and lethargic, while protein makes you feel uncomfortable and tense, opt for a fruit breakfast which is very unlikely to produce either of these adverse effects.

Apple and fig delight

Prepare this the evening before and chill it overnight. It is rich in both magnesium and zinc, as well as vitamin A and C.

> 1 large juicy eating apple
> ½ a medium grapefruit
> 2 stewed figs
> a little grated lemon peel
> 1 tbsp pumpkin seeds

Slice the apple roughly into a dish, leaving the peel on. Scrape the flesh from the grapefruit half, and add it to the apple, with all the juice this produces. Add the figs and a little of the water in which they were stewed. Mix in the grated lemon peel, and scatter over the pumpkin seeds.

Calorie count: about 230.

Crafty canteloupe

Canteloupe melon abounds among the breakfast recipes in this book. This is because it is rich in pyridoxine (vitamin B 6), and is a very convenient way of taking this nutrient in its natural form at the start of a day, when you do not feel like eating other foods which contain it (see below). Vitamin B 6 is of special use to you if you suffer from PMS. I have called this recipe 'crafty' because its sauce effectively disguises the wheat germ that accompanies it.

large slice of canteloupe melon
3 tbsp fresh raspberries or 3 tbsp raspberries tinned in juice
1 dsp wheat germ
2 tsp rosehip syrup
1 tbsp pumpkin seeds (optional)

Discard the melon seeds, and put the melon slice in a small dish.

Mash the raspberries with a fork, saving all their juice, and mix in the wheat germ. Add the rosehip syrup, stir, and pour this raspberry sauce over your melon. Add a tablespoon of pumpkin seeds if you like.

Calorie count: about 175 without the pumpkin seeds, about 325 with them.

If you whizz up all the above ingredients in your blender with 15 fl oz/450 ml skimmed milk, the resulting milk shake will then also be rich in vitamin B 12, very useful if you get period pains. The calorie count would then be 325 without the pumpkin seeds, and 475 with them.

Other breakfast recipes that would be suitable to you, include Egg energizer (page 33), rich in the vitamin E and calcium you need for menopausal symptoms; Apricot Astarte, (page 35), rich in the folic acid which can help period pains; and Super-porridge (page 63), providing oats to soothe your nerves as well as B 6 in the molasses and calcium in the milk.

Soya milk breakfast (page 34) and nut milks are also valuable for feminine problems. Their tryptophan content helps with menstrual discomfort, as well as tension and irritability, while the phenylalanine content of the nut milks produces brain tyrosine to help with depression.

Moody muesli, mark 7

The two main cereal ingredients in this muesli are oats and wheat germ, mainly because the former is a nerve tonic and the latter supplies vitamin E. The muesli as a whole is, of course, basically complex, unrefined carbohydrate, and the benefit of the tryptophan it releases into the brain has already been discussed above.

It also helps in a big way to guard against hypoglycaemia, as its sugar content is released slowly into the bloodstream, and the fibre it contains provides the roughage you need to remain free from constipation. This is especially important during periods, when menstrual discomfort can be aggravated by a full bowel.

2 tbsp porridge oats
1 tbsp wheat germ
1 tbsp pumpkin seeds
2 tsp rosehip syrup
3 or 4 dried apricots, chopped
1 dried fig, chopped
1 grated eating apple

Mix all the ingredients together. Soak overnight with 5 fl oz/150 ml of either skimmed milk or grapefruit juice.

Calorie count: about 650 with either liquid.

Both cottage cheese and eggs are among the best ideas for protein breakfasts for you. Try the following recipe that combines the two.

Egg and cottage cheese scramble

2 eggs
little skimmed milk
salt and pepper
1 small tomato

2 oz/50 g cottage cheese
1 tbsp sprouted alfalfa seeds

Scramble the eggs with a drop of skimmed milk. Season with the salt and pepper. Chop the tomato and add it with the cottage cheese to the scramble. Stir in the sprouted seeds immediately before serving. Eat this by itself, or with a piece of toasted corn bread (see below).

Calorie count: about 270.

Corn bread

The type of flour used here is made from cornmeal or maize meal, rich in magnesium. The bread is a beautiful golden colour, and is also gluten-free. You will also get tryptophan from the soya flour. This recipe is adapted from Alan Long's recipe in *The Sunday Times Book of Real Bread* (Rodale Press Ltd).

6 oz/175 g maize or cornmeal
2 oz/50 g soya flour
2 tbsp wheat germ
1 tsp baking powder
1 tsp clear honey
7 fl oz/200 ml skimmed milk
1 beaten egg
1 tbsp corn oil

Mix the flours, wheat germ and baking powder, then add the honey, milk and egg. Mix until smooth, add the corn oil and stir well. Pour into a greased baking tin and bake at 200°C/400°F or gas mark 6 for about 45 minutes.

Calorie count: 1330 for the whole loaf; about 135 per slice.

Lunches

Here is a salad that should suit you very well if you are trying to cope with PMS. Although GLA is present in reasonable quantity only in breast milk and evening primrose seed oil (see page 19), at least we can provide the starter substance from which it is made, i.e. cis-linoleic acid. Here it is present in the safflower oil.

While this, like other nutrients, should be included in our daily diet and not just when symptoms occur, nevertheless when you are suffering from PMS is an excellent time to remind yourself of the necessity of the relevant nutrients.

Soya bean salad with shrimps

Besides the cis-linoleic acid, this salad provides tryptophan to calm irritable nerves (in the soya beans, sesame seeds and shrimps), vitamin B 6 in the cabbage and wheat germ, and folic acid and zinc in the pumpkin seeds.

4 spring onions
3 oz/75 g cooked soya beans
3 oz/75 g peeled fresh shrimps
2 tbsp grated fresh raw cabbage
1 tbsp pumpkin seeds
1 dsp sesame seeds, toasted
1 tbsp grated raw carrot
1 dsp wheat germ
cider yoghourt dressing (see page 184)

Cut the spring onions into bite-sized pieces and mix everything together. Add the dressing, and mix well in.

This salad is nice with a hardboiled egg, or a little low fat soft cheese mixed with a chopped garlic clove.

Calorie count: about 500 without the dressing.

This dressing does not contain salt, although you may add a little if you like, because the water retention characteristic of PMS is made worse by salt in the diet.

Cider yoghourt dressing

2 heaped tbsp plain yoghourt
2 tbsp cider
1 tbsp safflower oil
1 tsp clear honey
1 tbsp capers

Mix the cider, yoghourt and oil together well, and stir in the honey and capers. Season with a little black pepper.

Calorie count: about 180.

The following salad uses liver for tryptophan, folic acid and many of the B vitamins, as well as nuts and seeds for magnesium and cottage cheese for calcium. These nutrients are especially useful if you suffer from period pains.

Cottage cheese and liver brunch

2 oz/50 g cooked lamb's liver
3 heaped tbsp finely grated raw cabbage
1 oz/25 g wholewheat pasta, cooked
1 tbsp sprouted seeds, e.g. alfalfa
2 oz/50 g cottage cheese
2 medium tomatoes, chopped
1 dsp pumpkin seeds
1 dsp chopped Brazil nuts
1 tbsp raisins

Cut up the liver into very thin slivers, and mix with the grated cabbage, pasta, sprouted seeds, cottage cheese, chopped tomatoes, and the seeds, nuts and raisins. Sprinkle the parmesan cheese on top and eat with a little cider vinegar dressing (see page 40), some corn bread (page 182), and a piece of fresh fruit.

Calorie count: about 600.

You need as much vitamin E as you can get when you are approaching or going through the menopause. Brussels sprouts, broccoli, wheat germ, spinach and eggs all supply this nutrient, and they all figure in the following salad. It is also rich in magnesium.

Green dream salad

> 3 or 4 Brussels sprouts
> 2–3 oz/50–75 g broccoli tops
> handful fresh spinach
> 1 hard-boiled egg
> 6 or 7 radishes
> 1 medium tomato
> 4 or 5 spring onions
> avocado dressing (see below)

Wash and cut outside injured leaves and stalks off the Brussels sprouts, wash and trim the broccoli and wash and pick over the spinach leaves. Tear up the latter roughly, with your fingers, and place in a dish. Chop the broccoli to convenient sized pieces, and coarsely grate the sprouts. Mix these three vegetables together, add the sliced hard-boiled egg, radishes, and chopped tomato and spring onions. Eat with avocado dressing (below), and some corn bread (page 182).

Calorie count: about 150.

Avocado dressing

This is a beautiful green dressing. If you are watching your weight, use it very sparingly or substitute two tablespoons of chopped parsley and/or some watercress for the avocado pear. The pear provides folic acid, and the yoghourt, calcium.

½ medium avocado pear
2 tbsp plain yoghourt
1 dsp wheat germ
grinding of pepper
shaking of garlic salt
a little skimmed milk to mix

Scrape the flesh from the avocado half, and place in a blender with the yoghourt, wheat germ, pepper and garlic salt. Blend until the ingredients are amalgamated, then add a little skimmed milk, blending after each addition, until you have the desired consistency.

Calorie count: about 400.

Sandwiches

Here are some ideas for sandwich fillings. Use either corn or wholewheat bread, or try the oatmeal bread recipe on page 160. Good alternatives are rye bread, and pumpernickel, dark, moist and delicious (rye is rich in folic acid). Pumpernickel is particularly delicious with (sinful!) cream cheese; if you decide to indulge, try Boursin cheese with black pepper, also with skimmed milk soft cheese.

1 minced cooked steak, with a chopped tomato, some finely chopped chives, and a teaspoon of wheat germ (lots of zinc and vitamin C for PMS).

2 watercress, with a hard-boiled egg, and some slices of yellow pepper, provide vitamins C, A and E for PMS.

3 sliced chicken liver, a little grated carrot, and some sprouted mung beans (i.e. bean shoots) with mayonnaise to give you iron, folic acid and tryptophan for painful periods.

4 mashed sardines, with a few finely chopped walnuts, a few drops of cider vinegar and cucumber slices (period pains).

5 mashed tinned salmon, with sunflower seeds, finely chopped Chinese cabbage and a sliced tomato to give calcium and magnesium for the menopause.

6 wheat germ, mashed into a hard-boiled egg with a little drop of safflower oil and malt vinegar, flavoured with Worcestershire sauce – vitamin E for menopausal symptoms.

Here is a pleasant-tasting soup that manages to incorporate all the nutrients mentioned in connection with menstrual and menopausal problems.

Lady-day soup

This is a cheering soup to drink hot at lunchtime, on a cold day, and it can also be enjoyed icy cold in summer. Try it with some freshly baked corn bread (page 182) and one of the above salads.

1 oz/25 g butter
1 tbsp safflower oil
1 bunch spring onions, chopped
2 grated carrots
1 small lettuce, shredded
large handful of watercress
1½ pints/900 ml stock made from a lamb bone
2 tbsp wholewheat flour
1 dsp wheat germ
a little white pepper
5 fl oz/150 ml skimmed milk
5 oz/150 g yoghourt
1 tbsp chopped fresh parsley

Melt the butter with the oil in a saucepan. Add the spring onions, carrots, lettuce and watercress and fry very gently for ten minutes. Stir in three quarters of the stock and simmer for another ten minutes, until the vegetables are tender. Blend the flour and wheat germ to a paste with the rest of the stock and blend into the soup. Season with the pepper and continue cooking until the soup has thickened. Purée everything in an electric blender, and if you are eating this soup hot, reheat and add the milk and yoghourt. If you are eating it cold, cool the soup after blending, and then stir in the milk and yoghourt. Sprinkle over the parsley. This will provide you with four servings.

Calorie count: about 220 per serving.

Evening Meal

Most women (and many men!) feel in distinct need of comfort when they arrive home from work – or surface from the day's debris created by housework, small children and treks to the supermarket. Men, however, do not have cyclical sexual/reproductive phases that make them feel in such dire need of solace and sympathy.

Two things, therefore, are required to make the evening at the end of a PMS/period discomfort/menopausal day something to look forward to. Any food preparation that has to be carried out must involve minimal labour. And the results of that preparation have to be both nutritious and delectable. Allowing for an inevitably wide spectrum of choice I have tried to make all the recipes in this final section both of these things.

Steak with herb butter

Whether you actually use butter or stick to margarine in this recipe does not really matter. Either will do, as the herbs disguise the flavour. However, butter is a little more luxurious. The steak is rich in tryptophan and phenylalanine.

1 × 6 oz/175 g fillet steak
a little safflower oil
lemon juice

Herb butter:

1 oz/25 g butter
1 tsp each of finely chopped fresh parsley, thyme and tarragon or half this quantity of the dried herbs
Worcestershire sauce

Mash the butter with the herbs and season lightly with Worcestershire sauce, mixing it in well. Put this in the freezer for a few minutes to harden. Meanwhile, brush the steak lightly with the oil and then the lemon juice, and grill to the degree of 'medium' or 'rare' or 'well done' that appeals to you. Serve the steak with the knob of herb butter on top (the contrasting temperatures are especially enjoyable). Eat with a warmed wholemeal roll, and some thinly sliced tomato, pepped up with a few drops of cider vinegar mixed with a teaspoon of clear honey and some more herbs.

Calorie count: about 510 with the herb butter.

Guava fast dessert

This could not be easier!

2 or 3 tinned guavas, in juice
about 12 to 15 seedless grapes
half a banana (make a milk shake in the morning with the rest)

Drain the guavas and place in a dish. Scatter the grapes and thickly sliced banana over them and moisten with the juice from the tin. Eat with 2 tablespoons of Greek strained yoghourt if you like.

Calorie count: about 100, without yoghourt, 140 with it.

Shrimp and asparagus omelette

This is rich in tryptophan and phenylalanine, and the mild flavour of the eggs and fish goes very well with spinach, and some new, minted potatoes.

2 eggs
1 tbsp water
little white pepper
little safflower oil
half a small tin of asparagus
3 oz/75 g peeled shrimps

Mix the eggs with the tablespoon of water and season lightly with the pepper. Lightly oil your omelette pan, heat, and pour in the beaten eggs. Push the runny eggs towards the centre of the pan as you tilt it from side to side, with a wooden spatula. Drain the asparagus (the water is delicious in soup), and place half the asparagus spears on the omelette together with the shrimps, when the omelette is nearly done. Fold one half over to cover the filling.

Chop the asparagus up first if you want, but this tends to be an 'untidy' omelette, more than compensated for by its flavour.

Melon fruit salad

Good old melon again! It is an excellent 'combiner' with other fruit; its copious supply of juice also makes it one of the most refreshing fruits in the world.

large slice of water melon
one small orange
small bunch of black cherries when in season or half a
small can of cherries in juice
1 tsp brown sugar
½ tsp powdered ginger or cinnamon

Scrape the flesh from the melon slice and discard the seeds. This can be a bit fiddly, as they go down so deeply into the flesh, but personally I like their flavour and crunchiness! Place melon pieces and all the juice that runs out in a small dish. Peel and cut up the orange, also conserving all the juice, and add to melon. Mix in the cherries, and scatter over the sugar and spice. If possible, chill before eating.

Calorie count: about 130 using fresh cherries, and 160 using canned.

Cauliflower cheese special

Cauliflower cheese is a good old standby, and the most obvious thing to offer a vegetarian visitor if you do not normally cook vegetarian foods. However, this recipe is for one very hungry person, or two with average appetites.

> 1 small cauliflower
> 3 oz/75 g mushrooms
> 1 oz/25 g margarine
> 1 tbsp wholewheat flour
> 10 fl oz/300 ml skimmed milk
> 1 level dsp fresh chives
> ½ tsp mustard powder
> 2 oz/50 g Edam or Gouda cheese
> 2 oz/50 g strong cheddar
> 2 level tbsp wholewheat breadcrumbs
> 1 tbsp parmesan cheese

Prepare the cauliflower and cook until tender but still fairly firm (crunchy, in fact, is even better for you if you like it like this). Wash and cut up the mushrooms. Melt the margarine, stir in the flour to a smooth paste, gradually add the milk, stirring constantly. Cook for 3 or 4 minutes until the sauce has thickened, add the cheeses and mustard powder and stir until the cheese has melted and the ingredients are well amalgamated. Add the chopped mushrooms and chives and pour over the cauliflower arranged in a lightly greased dish. Scatter over the wholewheat breadcrumbs and the parmesan cheese, and grill until the top is golden brown.

Calorie count: 1045.

Something cool and juicy goes well with this dish. I like some chunks of cucumber and freshly boiled beetroot, dressed with black pepper, and a little cider vinegar and honey.

Foamy fruit fool

You can use any fruit for this, preferably fresh. I am suggesting fruit canned in juice for this particular recipe, however, as the emphasis is on fast preparation. Rhubarb lends itself particularly well to this dessert.

> 1 large egg white
> 12 oz/350 g canned rhubarb in juice
> large pinch of ginger or cinnamon
> 5 oz/150 g plain yoghourt
> brown sugar to taste

Whisk egg white until stiff. Liquidize the fruit with the spice and a little of its juice in the blender, then add the yoghourt and blend again. Pour into a bowl and add sugar to taste if it needs this. Fold in the whisked egg white, and chill before eating. Serves two.

Calorie count: 165 per serving.

Here is a dinner party menu. While it is highly unlikely that all your guests will be in need of calcium, magnesium, vitamin E etc. for the treatment of period pains, PMS or menopausal symptoms, they will certainly be in need of these nutrients (and all the others that the recipes supply) for innumerable other metabolic reasons!

Egg castles

This is a pleasant and unusual starter. It also looks attractive, since the dark green of the watercress sets off the bright yellow egg yolk beautifully.

You need per person:

1 thick slice of fresh corn (page 182) or wholemeal bread
a little butter for spreading
1 large fresh egg
a little salt
black pepper
paprika pepper
handful of watercress

Toast the bread very lightly. Place on a baking tray, and gently scoop out a hollow in the centre of the slice of toast, using a teaspoon. Be careful not to go right through the toast to the other side. Spread the surface of the toast around the hollow with a little butter. Break the egg and separate it, save the white, and place the yolk, very gently so as to avoid breaking it, in the hollowed out toast centre. Whisk the egg white with a small pinch of salt and a grinding of black pepper until stiff and glossy, and then pile it on top of the egg yolk and toast, covering them completely and heaping up the egg white over the yolk to resemble a castle. Top with a shaking of paprika, and bake in an oven preheated to 180° C/350°F or gas mark 4 for about ten minutes or until the meringue is firm and golden (the yolk should be cooked but runny).

Serve at once, on white plates, surrounding the Egg castles with a ring of fresh watercress.

Calorie count: about 210 per serving.

Chicken with coriander

You are supplying your guests with plenty of tryptophan and phenylalanine when you cook this dish. But beware telling them too much about the excellent nutrients in the food they are consuming. Too analytical an approach to food actually in front of you can reduce the appetite considerably!

For each person:
>one quarter of a medium chicken
>1 oz/25 oz butter or margarine, softened
>very little salt (not for anyone with PMS)
>black pepper
>1 dsp fresh lemon juice
>1 tsp lemon rind, grated
>1 to 2 tsp coriander seeds

Wipe the chicken quarter with a damp cloth and pick off any feathery bits. Mash the butter or margarine with the salt if you are using it, the black pepper, the lemon juice and the lemon rind. Add the coriander seeds and mix them in well. Cover the chicken quarter all over with this mixture, and grill at a gentle to medium heat until cooked through. You can test this by piercing a thick part of the flesh and watching the colour of the juice. It is colourless when cooked, pink while still underdone. Serve with all the buttery sauce and juice that gathers in the pan, together with any coriander seeds that have rolled off the meat.

Coriander chicken is nice with some spinach or broccoli, some courgettes, and some potato mashed with a little milk.

Calorie count: about 510 for a chicken portion providing 6 oz/150 g meat.

Pears in red wine

This is a pleasant – and pretty – dessert with which to finish.

Per person:
>1 large, firm, ripe pear
>2 cloves
>piece of lemon peel
>medium or sweet red wine
>1 dsp clear honey

Peel the pear carefully, leaving its stalk on. Crush the clove heads, and push them into the pear in its wider end. Place the pear in a deep saucepan, together with the lemon peel, and cover with red wine. Add the honey, cover the saucepan and simmer gently until the pear is tender but still intact. Serve warm or chilled, accompanied by the winey juice.

NB It is difficult to give an exact amount of wine in this recipe, as it depends on how many pears are being used, the size of the saucepan etc. The calorie count per serving is worked out allowing about 5 fl oz/150 ml red wine with the fruit.

Calorie count: about 210.

Some Good Sources of Essential Brain Nutrients

Glucose

Derived both from natural sugars and from starches. Fruit sugar, syrups (e.g. maple), molasses; honey; many vegetables (e.g. root vegetables, especially carrots, parsnips, potatoes, sweet potatoes, yams). Wholegrain cereals, pulses and nuts; sun dried fruits, e.g. peaches, apricots, raisins, sultanas, currants; seeds, especially sunflower, pumpkin and pine kernels. Milk and its products.

Protein

Red meat (lamb, beef); poultry; offal; fish; eggs. Grains, especially wholewheat flour and its products (pasta, bread), wheat germ, oatmeal, soya flour and tofu. Pulses (e.g. butter beans, haricot beans, chick peas); nuts; dairy products, including milk, cheeses and yoghourt derived from cows', ewes' and goats' milk. See page 16 for information about how to combine grains, nuts and pulses to derive the full complement of essential amino acids.

Fats

Polyunsaturated fats, e.g. soya bean oil, safflower and sunflower oil, nuts and the oils derived from them (e.g. walnut, ground nut oil). Oily fish (e.g. salmon, herring, mackerel, pilchards, sardines, whitebait, sprats). Saturated fats, e.g. meat, milk and cream and their products. Certain vegetables, e.g. avocado pears (provide both saturated and unsaturated oils).

Fibre

Whole grains and their products; pulses; fruit, including dried fruit; nuts and vegetables.

Vitamins

Vitamin A

Fish and fish oil; liver; egg yolk; yellow fruit; all coloured vegetables, especially carrots, and the green leafy variety; margarine; milk and dairy products.

Vitamin B1 (thiamine)

Beef, pork, poultry; many vegetables, especially green leafy vegetables and pulses; oatmeal; whole grain cereals; bran; wheat germ; soya flour, soya milk and tofu; millet; yeast and yeast extracts; milk and milk products. Brazil nuts and peanuts.

Vitamin B2 (riboflavin)

Liver and kidney; fish, eggs; yeast and yeast extracts; green leafy vegetables; wholegrain cereals; milk and dairy products.

Vitamin B3 (niacin)

Lean meat, poultry, liver and kidney; fish; yeast and yeast extracts; whole cereals (especially wheatgerm, bran and wholewheat flour); nuts, especially peanuts; pulses; dried peaches.

Vitamin B5 (pantothenic acid)

Red meat, kidney, liver and heart, poultry; whole grains, especially the bran and wheat germ of wholewheat; nuts; yeast; unrefined molasses. Many green vegetables.

Vitamin B6 (pyridoxine)

Red meat, especially beef, kidney, liver and heart; eggs; yeast and yeast extracts; whole grains, especially wholewheat, bran and wheat germ; soya flour and its products, e.g. tofu, soya milk; some fruit (canteloupe melons, bananas); cabbage, sweet potatoes; nuts.

Vitamin B12 (cobalamin)

Red meat (beef, pork), liver, kidney and heart; eggs; milk and its products; yeast extract.

Choline (member of vitamin B complex)

Offal (liver, heart and brain); yeast and yeast extracts; eggs; green leafy vegetables; lecithin.

Inositol (member of vitamin B complex)

Beef liver, heart and brains; yeast and yeast extracts; wheat germ; dried lima beans; citrus fruit, especially grapefruit; canteloupe melon; molasses; nuts, especially peanuts; cabbage.

Octacosanol
Wheat germ oil.

Vitamin C
Citrus fruit, acerola cherries, blackcurrants, canteloupe melon, tomatoes, potatoes and sweet potatoes, cauliflower, green and leafy vegetables, e.g. cabbage, broccoli, calabrese, green (and red) peppers, courgettes, spring greens, sorrel, nettles, spinach and lettuce.

Vitamin E
Whole grain cereals and products, especially the wheat germ of whole wheat. Soya flour and its products, e.g. soya milk, tofu, soya sauce. Some green leafy vegetables such as Brussel sprouts, spinach, sorrel, nettles, broccoli and calabrese. Eggs.

Folic acid (vitamin M)
Meat, liver, poultry; eggs; fish. Yeast and yeast extracts; whole grains, especially wheat germ and bran from whole wheat; green leafy vegetables, especially the dark green ones such as spinach, watercress, broccoli and calabrese, sorrel, nettles and parsley.

Minerals

Calcium
Milk and milk products; whole grain cereals and their products; pulses, especially soya beans and its products, e.g. soya milk, tofu, soya sauce; certain fish, e.g. salmon, sardines; green vegetables; sunflower seeds; certain nuts, especially peanuts and walnuts.

Magnesium
Whole grain cereals, sweet corn (corn on the cob), maize flour; pulses; nuts, especially almonds; seeds; dark green vegetables, e.g. spinach, broccoli and calabrese, green peppers, sorrel, nettles, watercress, parsley; fruit, especially grapefruit, lemons, apples and figs; cocoa and chocolate.

Iron
Red meat and kidneys, liver and heart; pulses, especially soya beans and its products (soya flour, soya sauce, soya milk, tofu); whole grain cereals, especially oatmeal, wheat germ and bran from wheat, and millet; sago, tapioca, arrowroot; nuts; some seafood, especially clams and oysters; green vegetables, especially asparagus, parsley, spinach, broccoli, sorrel, nettles; eggs; molasses; dried peaches and dried figs; yeast and yeast extracts.

Potassium

Meat; milk and milk products; vegetables, especially potatoes, tomatoes, pumpkin, artichokes all green leafy vegetables, including mint leaves and watercress; seeds, especially sunflower; fruit, especially citrus fruit, avocado pears, honeydew melon, peaches, nectarines, plums, prunes, bananas, raisins and sultanas; walnuts.

Zinc

Meat, especially liver; seafood; low fat dried milk powder; whole milk and its products; whole grains, especially wheat and its products, including wheat germ and bran; oatmeal; nuts, especially almonds, Brazil nuts, walnuts, peanuts; eggs; yeast and yeast extracts; pumpkin seeds; mustard powder.

Selenium

Seafood; whole grains, especially whole rice, wheat germ and bran; onions, tomatoes, mushrooms, broccoli and calabrese; soya beans, tofu, soya sauce and soya milk. (The selenium content of vegetable sources depends upon their having been grown on soil rich in this mineral).

Sulphur

Beef; eggs; pulses; fish; cabbage and some other green vegetables.

Amino Acids

Tryptophan

Beef, lamb, liver, chicken, especially the breast; some fish, especially trout and cod; shrimps; some pulses, especially soya beans and its products (soya flour and milk, soya sauce, tofu); skimmed milk, cottage cheese; nuts, especially Brazil nuts and roasted peanuts; seeds, especially sesame and pumpkin.

Phenylalanine

All the above mentioned sources of tryptophan are also good sources of phenylalanine; others include lima beans, chick peas, almonds and walnuts.

Histidine

Turkey, veal, chicken; eggs; non-fat milk and cottage cheese; peanuts and peanut butter.

Arginine

Beef, turkey, chicken; dried non-fat milk and cottage cheese; haddock, halibut; shredded wheat cereal; red kidney beans; peanuts and peanut butter, pecan nuts, walnuts.

Nucleic Acids

Chicken liver; fish, especially anchovies, salmon and sardines; wheat germ and bran, oatmeal; some pulses including lentils and pinto beans; vegetables, including mushrooms, asparagus and spinach.

Superoxide Dismutase (SOD)

This enzyme is present in all the raw fruits and vegetables we normally include in our diets. The best sources of SOD are, therefore, salads that include a wide selection of ingredients, both vegetables and fruit, seeds, nuts and sprouting seeds. Freshly prepared fruit and vegetable juices are also an excellent source.

Index

almonds
  milk shake with figs 138
  nut milk 34
  restorative milk shake 119
'Aphrodite's dream' dessert 172
apples
  apple and fig delight 179
  apple snow 78
  baked with fruity filling 105
apricot Astarte 35
asparagus 130

banana
  custard 129, 167
  milk shake 62
beef
  beany casserole 50
  beef tea 147
  steak tartare and alfalfa sprouts 140
  steak with herb butter 188
blackcurrant summer pudding 153
bread
  alfalfa sprout and wheat germ soda bread 141
  corn bread 182
  milk baps 120
  oatmeal and walnut muffins 64
  oatmeal bread 91, 160
  wholewheat and pumpkin seed bread 36
bread and butter pudding 131

cake, lunch 101
cauliflower cheese 129
  special 191
chicken
  homely casserole 109
  with coriander 193
citrus fruit compôte 62
citrus surprise, hot 137
cod and prawn parcels 44
cottage cheese
  brunch with liver 184
  on toast 93
  scrambled 181
curry, vegetable 77

dressings
  avocado 185
  basil mayonnaise 163
  basil vinaigrette 162
  cider vinegar 40
  cider yoghourt 184
  green garlicky 96
  horseradish 144
  lemon, honey and herb 68
  lemony yoghourt 143
  red wine and caper vinaigrette 70
  yoghourt and chervil 122

eggs
  breakfast 36, 119
  coated with pilchards 98
  coddled 120
  egg castles 192
  energizer drink 33
  enhancer drink 159
  kippered 93
  scrambled with cottage cheese 181

figs
  apple and fig delight 179
  milk shake with almonds 138
  stewed with raisins and pistachio nuts 149
fish cakes 65
fish supper, rapid 148
'floating clouds' dessert 52
fruit fool, foamy 192
fruit salad
  Aphrodite's dream 172
  melon 190
  rapid 76
  with cashew nut cream 150

game creams 130
gooseberry and avocado delice 110
guava fast dessert 189

haddock, breakfast 120
hearts, stuffed 103
herrings in oatmeal 102

juice
  apple, pear and carrot 88
  beetroot and onion 137
  broccoli and Brussels sprout 158
  carrot, beetroot and cucumber 117
  carrot and celery 117
  carrot and celery delice 61
  radish 137
  raspberry, blackberry and raisin 178
  spinach, carrot and celery 32, 89
  St Clement's cocktail 60
  tomato 137
  tomato sunrise 60
junket 46

kidneys
  on toast 139
  pâté, liver or kidney 71
  soup 151
kippered eggs 93
kippers 92

lamb
  chops with sage 75
  roast with coriander 80
liver
  breakfast grill 160
  brunch with cottage cheese 184
  herby casserole 46
  pâté, liver or kidney 71
  scrambled with wheat germ 140

melon
  Charantais melon lake 107
  crafty canteloupe 179
  crunchy starter 158
  fruit salad 190
  momento melon 33
  orange and melon jelly 49
  with banana 118
milk shakes
  almond restorative 119
  banana 62
  fig and almond 138
muesli, moody 35, 65, 90, 119, 141, 161, 181

nut milk 34, 119, 138

oatmeal
  bread 91, 160
  herb oatcakes 97
  macaroons 76
  muffins with walnuts 64
  possett 82
  super-porridge 63
omelette, shrimp and asparagus 189
onions, stuffed 149
orange and melon jelly 49
oysters, for starters 170

pancakes, orange 74
pasta
  easiest spaghetti 169
  macaroni coleslaw salad 123
  salad with anchovies 69
  salad with shrimps 164
pastry, wholemeal 106
peaches
  peach amazement 89
  peachy yoghourt crunch 103
  with strawberry sauce 168
pears in red wine 194
pilchard eggs 98
porridge, super 63
pulses and grains, cooking 38

quiche, spinach and mushroom 105

rosé dessert 81

salads
  barley winter 143
  buckwheat, radicchio and celeriac 68
  bulgur wheat, beetroot and greenery 40
  butter bean, spinach and anchovy 162
  chick pea and spinach 67
  English 97
  excelsior layered 151
  flageolet with bean shoots and green beans 95

green dream 185
green vitality 123
lima bean 39
macaroni coleslaw 123
millet and smoked oyster 94
pasta with anchovies 69
pasta with shrimps 164
pulse 68
soya bean, alfalfa and tofu 142
soya bean with shrimps 183
sweetcorn, bean and tuna 122
tarragon rice 41
tomato and green pepper 169
turkey, bulgur wheat and endive 163
salmon bake 73
sandwiches 42, 70, 99, 124, 145, 164, 186
seasame toasts 50
soup
  broccoli 100
  Brussels sprout 126
  kidney 151
  Lady-day 187
  nettle 108
  onion and potato 125
  relaxation broth 72
  South American 49
  spiced black-eyed bean 146
  spicy lentil 43
  summer apricot 79
  watercress 165
soya milk breakfast 34
spaghetti, easiest 169
sponge fruit pudding 128
stuffing, herb and garlic 171
sweetbreads, sautéed 127

tahini sauce 48
tea
  basil 157
  herbal 59
  lemon balm 31
  raspberry leaf 157
tomatoes, baked 45
trout, grilled with nutty potatoes 167
tuna, sweetcorn and bean salad 122
turkey
  bulgur wheat and endive salad 163
  scrambled 159

veal
  loin with herb and garlic stuffing 171
  with soft cheese 166
vegetarian stir-fry, quick, 47

Welsh rarebit, boozy 125
whiting, steamed 128

yoghourt surprise 47

Index compiled by Peva Keane